House Officer At The Brigham
1965-1966
How I Got Through It

Richard B. Whiting, MD

Contents

PROLOGUE

My motives for writing this book are several. Primarily, this offers me the opportunity to express deepest gratitude to the Peter Bent Brigham Hospital and its staff, physicians, and other trainees who contributed to a profound learning experience in all of medicine. I also believe it is worthwhile to describe life as a medical house officer in 1965-66 at one of the premier centers for medical research and education. In many ways, the experiences back then at most medical centers were extreme. Over time considerable changes in medical education developed at least in part fostered by litigation such as the Libby Zion case of 1984 in which house staff long hours were at least partially causal for that patient's poor care. Accepted guidelines for residency training evolved considerably in the direction of improved working and learning conditions as well as the expected improvement in overall patient care. Today, the Accreditation Council of Graduate Medical Education(ACGME) publishes detailed guidelines for all types of medical and surgical residency training and rigorously reviews training programs for compliance. In 1965 resident hours were too long, time off too short, responsibility often beyond expertise, and of course salaries were dismal. In the past 55 years medical education has changed and all medical science has dramatically changed as well. In a broad sense, clinical practice is constantly in a state of evolution as new scientific data is added and old concepts discarded. For the purposes of this memoir, I must point out the passage of time has taken a heavy toll on my efforts to find details to augment my 80-year-old memory bank supported in part by the extensive archives of Harvard Medical School, the Countway Medical Library, and Brigham and Women's Hospital. Very many cherished colleagues and mentors have died or are disabled. My darling wife, Johnalin, played a huge role in this story and she also has died leaving a huge hole in my life but also eliminating her perspective as devoted wife of a medical house officer in that era. As it turned out, the fact that she shared so much with me at that time produced another reason for me to put together this story. The story of the time at the Brigham, the engagement in education and experience, the hardships, and life itself in Boston all were intermingled with a young couple with a small infant moving

1

far away from family and friends and making a new life by simply having a very close loving relationship. The fact is I benefited enormously by the loving understanding of that wonderful woman and that markedly contributed to my ability to tolerate the hours, the stress, and the anxiety of that high powered environment.

There were 13 of us in the house officer class of 1965-66. The Brigham was very well known and able to recruit from the very top of medical school graduates for their house officer positions. The custom was to select 6 directly from Harvard Medical School and the other 7 from other schools all over the country.

The medical house officers selected for 1965 were:

- William H. Barry from HMS
- Bruce A. Chabner from HMS
- George U. Fisher from HMS
- William Grossman from Yale School of Medicine
- Martin F. Kagnoff from HMS
- Arthur Kales from U. of Chicago Medical School
- John C. LaRosa from Pittsburg Medical School
- David M. Livingston from Tufts Medical School
- Glenn L. Melson Il from Washington U. School of Medicine
- Abraham Potolsky from SUNY Downstate College of Medicine
- Richard Selden from HMS
- Ralph W. Stoll from HMS
- Richard B. Whiting from St Louis U. School of Medicine

I gratefully acknowledge help with this memoir from Drs. Barry, Chabner, Grossman, LaRosa, and Livingston.

The actual physical plant of the Brigham was unusual as it involved a main building and entrance connected to all other parts of the facility by a very long corridor called "The Pike". Originally it was thought this corridor should be open to the air which would help prevent spread of disease by reason of open air and some sunlight.

Over time this protection was not found to really matter so this path from entrance to the last ward(F main)was completely enclosed thus replacing an ivy bordered sidewalk with a long-enclosed corridor with one wall nearly all large windows. This was the Pike we knew in 1965, and I believe it was approximately one quarter mile in length. This design played a definite role in the experiences of all house staff and others. This was re-enforced in my mind by one of my colleagues who described to me his first night as a medical house officer included multiple long trips through the distal end of the Pike to the blood bank and then back to F main in the care of a man with severe gastro-intestinal bleeding. Thus, the Pike always played some role in day-to-day activities. The Pike gave off branches to all medical and surgical areas but also to the radiology department, the laboratories, blood bank, cafeteria, many offices, and at its beginning right at the hospital main entrance there was a small café that was popular and by way of a staircase led out to the courtyard with Harvard Medical School and the Countway Medical Library. On the second floor of the hospital entrance was the Department of Medicine and one floor above that was the house staff quarters. The latter were spartan in size and décor but did provide a room with a bed and usually a small table with a lamp for any time a member of house staff could leave the immediate area of his ward responsibility.

The vastness of this hospital complex coupled with the separation of the various patient areas that we all dealt with meant there was a somewhat low likelihood of house officer comradery. As a group we were competitive by nature. There was good bonding for the pair of house officers that alternated call with each other for the year but otherwise I at least usually felt that I hardly knew members of the group. I do think the graduates in our group from Harvard Med School had somewhat of an advantage in this regard as they were totally familiar with the physical plant of hospital and surroundings, knew each other, and knew many of the faculty, other residents, and rotating students. As I learned much later, many of my co-house officers actually lived very near the Brigham. In some cases, wives could bring over a meal for their husband who was on call in the hospital. As I will describe later, moving to Boston from St Louis, Johnny and I had help in finding a home, but it was far from the hospital which like many things in life presented both positive and negative side effects.

CHAPTER ONE: Arrival and First Rotation

The highway scenery flew past my window. We were headed East to Boston for my residency at The Peter Bent Brigham Hospital. The Brigham had been recognized for years as a source of meaningful research as well as outstanding clinical education. Once I was there, I did hear a few somewhat crude remarks about being at the "bent peter" but on this particular ride my mind was filled with much more sober thoughts. Those thoughts usually started with the realization how I got to this point.

Even in my medical school days, I became aware of the incredible impact on all of medicine by Harvard Medical School together with its group of closely affiliated hospitals particularly the Peter Bent Brigham. During all of my early years in med school I was totally engrossed in my studies and obsessed with science as applied to medical care. I gave little thought to my future in medicine and I think I just assumed that I would finish school and remain in the St Louis area for my career. During my third year when I became much more closely involved with medical care including all the major specialties of medicine and surgery, I realized there would be several important choices that I would have to make within months. The first of these turned out to be easy as my rotations as a junior through all the basic categories of possible future activities boiled down to a clear feeling that I was much more attuned to medical type practice than one that was surgical in type. Of course, one of the big decisions was where to apply for post graduate medical training-internship and residency. This was a very common topic of discussion among all of my fellow students and hearing their plans and ideas served to make me start to consider opening up all my possible ideas for future training to include areas outside of the St Louis region. One thought that I had was that if I went away from St Louis University Med School that would mean exposure to an entirely different group of teachers and mentors. The idea of training with a different group of clinicians from those I already really liked would open up much more diversity in my thinking. In the course of thinking about the unlikely idea that I would go well away from St Louis, I still never really thought about the Boston area and Harvard affiliated hospitals. That changed surprisingly due to my own chairman of medicine, Dr Thomas Frawley who was a highly respected endocrinologist and who often cited the eastern schools especially Harvard and in particular fact he often talked about the Peter Bent Brigham Hospital with a lot of positive comments. When I was on my junior year rotation in Internal Medicine and assigned to the university hospital medical service, I had a lot of contact with Dr Frawley. He was a good teacher and very knowledgeable but seldom issued any kind of compliments. There came a point during one of his rounds that I indicated some interest in a residency like the one at the Brigham hospital and he slid into comments that I shouldn't think about that as it was far outside my reach. That comment really bothered me and it led me to find time to visit the medical library there at SLU to see what I could learn about the Peter Bent Brigham Hospital in Boston. Alas! There was no internet! By using the Index Medicus and tracking some articles about health care and medical training I managed to find a few bits and pieces about that hospital that definitely served to pique my interest. I discovered that the chairman of surgery at the Brigham was Dr Francis D. Moore who also was the editor and lead author of the textbook of surgery most used by medical schools including my own. I had read much of that book when I was on my junior year rotation on surgery service. The chairman of the Medicine Department at the Brigham I learned was Dr George W. Thorn who was a highly noted endocrinologist often quoted by my own chairman of medicine. There were several other bits of information that I discovered and found to be really of interest. The first successful renal transplant had been done at the Brigham, the first use of the Iron Lung for polio victims, and several seemingly very advanced forms of cardiac surgery for valvular heart disease. So, I have to admit there was a sort of fledgling interest on my part in the possibility of aiming high and actually applying for the house officer position at the Brigham. This was the place where serendipity came into this entire thought process as I met Dr Eugene Lewis who was on the faculty and one of the attendings. Dr Lewis had graduated from Harvard Medical School and completed most if not all of his post graduate training in the Boston area. He had a delightful dialect with Bostonian overtones and was very charismatic, very well liked by all the students. I myself, was totally enamored by this man primarily because he gave off an aura of truly caring for the patients, each and every one. I remember being so impressed with this man that I went home and told my wife, Johnny, details of my encounters with him. Johnny and I were married just before the start of my sophomore year in med school and by this time had made lots of adjustments to married life together with her work schedule during the day plus my variable work hours including nights and regular call schedule. In addition, she was amazing in that she easily let me spend long hours studying and at the same time was very eager to hear about my day. As my very effective sounding board, she picked up immediately on the idea that continuing my education in a new environment especially one with a very solid reputation, would provide me some very rich experiences. We both immediately vocalized the enormous difficulty involved in a major move from St Louis simply because it would mean leaving all that was familiar to us as well as family and friends. That realization plus the feeling that I really wouldn't get such an opportunity led both of us to more or less forget the idea of going somewhere like Boston. I now and then thought of training in such a place more or less as the kind of "fun" thinking one does at quiet times. As one would expect, the day-to-day activities for both of us filled our time and nearly all of the discussion about travel, training, and moving fell away.

It didn't take long before the time came to actually fill out applications for residency programs and looking at those forms and thinking about where I would want to devote a chunk of our lives for training actually brought back the rush of that idea:what if I did get to move to an excellent center for some of my training? The readers of this memoir can see what's coming. More or less as a lark I sent in applications for house officership at two of the Boston facilities, The Massachusetts General Hospital and the Peter Bent Brigham Hospital. Obviously, I applied to several hospitals in the St Louis area and in fact St Louis U let me know I would be given a spot if I wanted it.

Back then and continued through the years to the present ,applicants went through the process of application using the National Residency Matching Program. The schools and hospitals looking to fill their rosters of house officers also were in that same system. The concept was to use the computer to match up as close as possible the applicants who listed their top choices with the programs who listed their top candidates. That way a lot of the confusion of selection for potential residents and the highest possible number of matches were made that satisfied both candidate and institution.

I did interview at several places in St Louis and easily could form a ranking of my choices. To my great surprise, I received a letter informing me that I was invited to come to Boston for interviews at both the places that I had applied. My first reaction was immense excitement but that was soon tempered by the thought that the whole application on my part had been somewhat of a lark. I probably would not get in, and finally we couldn't manage the cost of visiting Boston for the interviews. I showed the letter to Johnny and of course she was thrilled for me, but by then, I was clearer and so I said it would be nice but no way can we afford that interview trip. I was very surprised by her immediate response. At that time, she was the breadwinner for us as she had a very good job at KMOX-TV as continuity director and she said we certainly could afford that trip and in fact she thought I should go. She indicated that if I did not take that invitation and did not go for interviews , I would very likely be sorry all the rest of my life. She pointed out I would always wonder what would have happened if I had taken the invitation. She thought we could afford the airfare to Boston and back and maybe we could find s relatively reasonable place for me to stay. Afterall there would be many others making similar trips. Over the next few days, I considered this whole idea. I had a good friend from my high school days, a Jesuit Priest, who had spent a lot of time in Boston and so I called him and explained my problem. He said he would look into it for me and call me back soon. Several days later he called me and indicated he did have a friend in Boston who would be willing to drive me around and let me stay at her home so I could go to the interviews at both hospitals. That lady was Mary McDonald who was a widow living in a small home with her son who was grown and employed although he was blind. This lady quickly became a sort of a saint for me and Johnny-see later.

All of this continued to run through my thoughts as we drove toward Boston. I was consumed by these and related thoughts about what we would encounter in the new life, how would we manage, would I measure up to the Ivy league standards of medical care and education, and other questions. It seemed that my mind kept taking me back to the events leading up to this drive. I recalled my previous trip to Boston for the interviews. As I indicated I now had a contact in Boston to help me accept the invitation for interviews in Mrs. Mary McDonald. She was wonderful. She picked me up at Logan Airport and was my official driver into Boston and to her home. I was given my own room and made to feel very welcome. I met Rod, her son who was also very nice. She provided great meals for me over my whole visit and as mentioned, she drove me the next morning to the Brigham for that set of interviews. The experiences of that day are still fairly clear in my mind. There was a very large group of students there that day for interviews. We all went through the same process which lasted most of that day. There were eight interview rooms set up with 1 to 3 examiners in each. I was ushered into each room in sequence and in each case, I was greeted by the principal examiner who introduced himself and others in the room. Very often there was some effort to allay my apprehension such as Dr Bert Valle a very active research scientist offering me a candy mint in case I needed it. In spite of over 56 years since that day, I still remember some of the questions asked of me. Dr Roger Hickler. the leader at the Brigham of the Hypertension Unit asked me how it could happen that a glass of red wine could markedly increase one's blood pressure that was previously controlled. As luck would have it, I had recently read a medical journal dealing with that very problem and so I could definitely answer that question. One of the examiners was the Chief of Medicine himself, Dr George W. Thorn and he asked me what I would think about a patient who was an elderly lady walking along the street and when she stepped down off the curb she immediately heard a strange soft crack noise and felt pain in her hip causing her to fall to the ground. I understood he was getting at a fracture of the hip from very minor trauma and thus was asking why that could happen. This was an active area of research dealing with decreased bone strength with ageing due to one or more common causes of abnormal calcium homoeostasis, weakened muscle support of an ageing limb, or possibly some sort of hormonal imbalance not to mention simple osteoporosis. This led me to discuss some of what I could recall about these issues. Nearly all of the questions asked of me that day were like these. They started with a brief clinical history and then led into what I should consider in the light of that history.

At the end of that day, I was drained. Mrs. McDonald picked me up and we drove back to her home for dinner. We visited for a while, and she asked me a lot about my family and also my wife. She let me go to my room to think or to sleep and told me she would call me in the morning for the ride to Massachusetts General Hospital for the second day of interviews. That whole day was similar to my first day of examinations and for whatever reason much of it is not as clear to me now. There was one interview that I seem to recall from that day. It was with a psychiatrist who welcomed me and told me to have a seat. We talked about stress and how people tried to cope with it. At one point he indicated the room felt stuffy so would I please go to the window and open it for some air. This is vague to me, but it seemed I could not open that window, but I could see the latch was not fixed. I gave up after a few tries and no more was said about the room being stuffy. There were of course a host of interviewers and many clinical type questions and once again the end of the interviews was associated with some relief and fatigue.

I believe Mary picked me up that afternoon and returned me to the airport to catch my flight home to St Louis. Johnny picked me up and we drove home, but she was loaded with questions about my trip. At that point I could say that I felt very glad that I had gone, and she agreed. I was thinking that I had seen a lot of both hospitals and was glad for that experience. I told her that after the second day of interviews, I briefly found my way to the Ether Dome at the MGH where ether had been first used in a human for elective surgery and that in fact both hospitals were loaded with old examples of medical history. She and I returned to our respective activities with no further discussion of the Boston area. Several of my co students knew of my trip and asked about the whole experience. But then, it all was forgotten as I was sure I would remain in St Louis for my residency.

Match day is at all med schools a very big day with a lot of excitement and often parties. This was true for St Louis University Medical School then as it is still today. As the matching announcement was gradually read there were some students who were delighted with their soon to be residency spots, some who seemed indifferent or merely heard confirmed what they had expected. I believe I was the one student who was most surprised when I heard my name and that I matched at the Peter Bent Brigham

Hospital in Boston. I was totally shocked! I was soon given some handshakes and slaps on the back from co students who understood a little of what that position meant. Johnny hugged me and kissed me with tears running down her cheeks. The partying began and after a while Johnny and I left to go home and tell our parents what had happened. Now we really started to consider what this match really meant for us. We had a baby daughter born in October of my senior year and she had become a focus for our whole family group. Many issues surfaced for us including finances as we already owed a chunk of money by way of student loans from the AMA ERF and The Missouri State Medical Foundation. We would need to move away from family and friends and all of their support. We couldn't fathom what type of stresses we would encounter with a very new life in Boston and the entirely new medical environment of my education.

Thoughts of graduation were delayed as we started to address the needs of the travel to Boston. I contacted Mary Mc Donald who was my only liason in the area and she graciously offered to find us a place to rent. As I will mention a little later, Mary did us big service in this regard as she found us a quiet street in a two-family home with the landlords living on second floor and we could rent the whole first floor. As the time to leave St Louis approached, we stored some things with our families and gave some things away. Johnny gave several weeks notice to her job with KMOX TV and her mother, Irma, volunteered to drive us to Boston. She had a fairly new big Oldsmobile with a rack on the top and located a vinyl white container that fit inside the rack with straps to fasten it in place. This allowed us to select the bare necessities to take with us like clothes, bed sheets, covers, towels, a few books, and a lot of baby things including a playpen for little Anne.

Irma drove the entire trip as far as I remember with me in the front passenger seat pouring over maps from Triple A. In the back seat, Johnny sat with our baby and on occasions nursed the baby while her little brother, Rob sat next to her close to the driver side window often playing with handheld games. Sometimes I came back to the raw fact that an application for a position I wanted but had completed on a lark, had resulted in the present travel and an enormous number of unknown events in our future life. The drive to Boston was a long one and most of it remains foggy to me today. I

11

know we stopped for overnight rest at least twice, but I have no recollection of where we stayed. My time in the car was used up by the need to follow the maps but also myriads of thoughts about how we got to this point, what it would be like in a new medical environment, whether I would measure up, how my little family would manage emotionally and particularly financially, and a continuous cascade of other concerns. Whenever I looked in the back seat, I would see Johnny playing with little Anne or nursing, or even dozing off but she always seemed at ease. Rob was young and maybe a little bored at the long ride but seemed otherwise OK with the trip. I focused on the fact that my residency would keep me away from Johnny and Anne a lot and my absence would be lonely time for Johnny. I think I made a little promise to myself to try to keep in mind what our new life would mean for my wife. Sometimes this led to my wondering "What have I done? "This could be very difficult for all three of us and also how would we be able to afford living in Boston. With my meager salary how would we manage unless we borrowed more money? The yearly salary for house officers at the Brigham had that very year gone up to $3,600.00. We were on our way to a new home but one we had never seen. We had of course by this time had some experience with rental properties and tight budgets during my second, third, and fourth year of medical school. There was a little hope that we could in fact get along as we had in St Louis. For me there was always some concern about my performance in a high-pressure type medical training program and a definite desire to not make St Louis U Med School look weak. This idea led to a slightly different train of thought about how I did feel that I had done everything I could have done to prepare for this new phase of my education. It is not my usual thought process, but I examined what I had done in med school to assuage some of this fear of performance. I had really studied often and very hard and did achieve very good grades. I had been lucky to have been inducted into the well-known honor medical society known as Alpha Omega Alpha and did that in my junior year. I remembered how much help and support I had gotten from my wife who actually helped me study.

The medical school curriculum at that time included two complete rotations through all the major categories of medicine and surgery: Internal Medicine, Surgery, Obstetrics-Gynecology, and Pediatrics with all their subsidiary sub sections. During the junior year all the students rotated through each area with a lot of reading, patient encounters, bedside teaching, and yes, a lot of so called "scut work". That means doing a lot of necessary little jobs to make the totality of patient care progress. This for example would include drawing blood, writing notes of all patient encounters, doing simple lab work which would include doing some simple blood tests, urine testing, and stool testing for evidence of occult blood as a sign of silent bleeding into the gastro-intestinal tract. There were in those days quite a few tests that a student could perform and over time fewer and fewer of these were needed except when a patient was admitted after regular lab people were off or in some way got sick during the night.

The second rotation through these areas of medicine and surgery, I was often listed as Acting Intern which meant I could with supervision write orders, be in charge of patient care, and become much more deeply involved in overall care. I thought this experience would really help me in internship as I would be more familiar with order writing and all that went into it.

These comments serve to paint a picture of what I was like going into this entirely new world and dragging my wife and daughter along with me. We all would be far from family, friends, and previous mentors and need to measure up to a host of obstacles.

Finally, we arrived in the Boston area and found our way to Harvard Square where we had reservations at the Holiday Inn. Once we were checked in and found our rooms, we all decided to take a short walk and explore the area. Harvard Square was bustling with activity and people. The college itself was there and Radcliffe College very nearby. There also was a major transit terminal where buses drove in from areas farther outside the city and dropped off passengers who then went about business in the Harvard Square area or more likely went downstairs to the MTA underground transit system-the subway which could then be taken to nearly any area of the large city of Boston. The area we walked around the Square was loaded with shops, a large Co-Op store for Harvard and other school employees, and some eating establishments. There were fruit stands, bookstores, and all kinds of small businesses. As I alluded to already, there were many people milling about like students, tourists, shoppers, etc. There is a sort of profound excitement within the area of Harvard Square and over all subsequent years in Boston, I always felt that same air of excitement as I visited the area.

The next day we were all awake early and had a light breakfast. We drove to the Peter Bent Brigham Hospital so I could sign in and pick up a packet of information for new house officers. The front of the hospital was really quite impressive with the actual main entrance and six huge colonnades set back from the intersection of Huntington Avenue and Francis Street. Inside the entrance I found a desk and reception area where I identified myself and was given the expected packet of papers to get me started on the house officership.

I returned to the car, and we drove down Francis Street and noticed how different the houses looked compared with St Louis. We returned to the hotel for lunch and so Johnny could nurse little Anne. I had already torn open the packet and started reading through the material provided. Riding in the car, I only skimmed the papers which indicated general information about the medicine service at the Brigham. Once we in our hotel room, I laid the papers on the table and started to really study them. I was stunned to learn that my call schedule was every other night and every other weekend! This schedule was different from my previous experience with call requirements since they had all been more regular and orderly like every third night or even every fourth night on duty. I think the paperwork did describe the important features of the Brigham schedule. In order to be off on a weekend, I would work all day and night Thursday and all-day Friday. The opposite was also spelled out: If you were on call on a weekend, you would then come home on Thursday night and Friday night before that weekend. It was not stated but I already knew that even on a day off, you never left your service until all your patient work was completed including all the notes in the chart. So, Johnny and I had become used to my sometimes-late return home even on a night off. She and I focused on the proposed call schedule and could feel each others anxiety. At that time, we still didn't believe that call schedule would last the entire year.

The next day Johnny's mom, Irma, drove us to the address I had been given by Mary McDonald and where we would live. It was on the outskirts of Boston in Arlington Heights. We of course didn't realize how far that actually was from the Brigham campus but we both assimilated that fact into our lives with all the other changes. The street was Surrey Rd, a typical quiet Boston neighborhood. Our new home was the first floor of a two-family house and the owners lived upstairs on the second floor. Mr. and Mrs. Walsh were remarkable, warm, loving people both with white hair and Boston background. Their son, Tom, lived with them and drove each day to work. Both Johnny and I, and I think also Irma, were quickly "taken" by the Walshes. None of us realized at the time of first arrival that the Walsh family would become very instrumental in our ability to manage living in Boston. Mrs. Walsh was a sweet lady and would soon take Johnny and Anne "under her wing". I was lucky to have Mrs. Walsh show Johnny some cooking tricks like how to make fabulous fish chowder. She provided some information about the neighborhood that was reinforced when Mary McDonald arrived to help us get settled. Between these two women we learned there was a small market, a laundry, a drug store, and even an ice cream parlor very near our new home.

Mary also brought a few items for us like a lamp, a few kitchen utensils, and one or two pictures to go on the wall. I guess both Johnny and I were overwhelmed by the amount of new information we got from these two women and in fact some of what was described to us we didn't really learn until later when we could actually walk the neighborhood.

We really didn't have very much that we had brought from St Louis, and it all was easily carried into the house and rearranged together with the items we were given by the Walshes and Mrs. McDonald.

Too soon, Johnny's mom and her brother, Rob, packed up and started their return trip to St Louis. So, the new Boston contingent of the Whiting family was all alone. Johnny was a little teary and held on to little Anne very close and I held them both. We realized we needed to be occupied so we checked out the small back yard and the patch of grass. Then the three of us decided to walk the area around our neighborhood. We went into the small family-owned store and looked over a very different but really nice store compared to anything from our past. There were many cheeses, sauces, fruits and many other food items that seemed appealing. We then found a small drug store and I bought a wind-up type clock with an alarm. Back to the house we surveyed our would-be living quarters. There was plenty of space but not much in the way of furniture or decor. Our clothes were folded and put in cardboard boxes on the floor of the bedroom, and we covered the mattress with a sheet that had made it with us from St Louis. The kitchen seemed fine with an ice box, stove, a small table, and two chairs plus some dishes, glasses, and a few kitchen utensils. The feeling that I remember the most from that day is that Johnny and I each felt a need to reassure the other. As I recall we only had one or two days together in the new home before the day arrived for me to go to the Brigham. That would be a big day for each of us since it would be the start of my year as a house officer and the start of her year of coping with loneliness. We made all sorts of possible plans trying to handle possible problems. We laid out the clothes I would need for the first day and Johnny planned to make me a good bag lunch with a few snacks since the eating arrangements at the hospital at that time were unknown. Finally, I set the alarm and we went to bed but neither of us could easily sleep so there was surely some expected anxieties hiding in both of us. Of course, the little one we dearly loved, Anne, also contributed to the lack of sound sleep that first night.

When the alarm went off, it was loud and metallic in timbre which reminded me of the opening bell for a major fight. I can now say, that was much more appropriate than I suspected at the time. I got The both of my "girls" very hard, I left the house headed for the nearby corner where the MTA Bus stopped. The first leg of that journey was a straight shot down Massachusetts Avenue to Harvard Square where the bus emptied and nearly all of us headed down into the subway station. I had been schooled in the way a tourist finds his or her way around Boston using the fabulous subway system. There was nothing like it in St Louis then or now. I knew the rough approach would include buying tokens, asking for directions, and carefully watching for signs. As I bought the tokens, I also asked the attendant how to reach the Peter Bent Brigham Hospital and she spelled it out for me. It turned out to be not too difficult as I would stay on the first train all the way to Symphony Station where I would get off and then go to the train headed for Brigham Circle. That was my actual destination.

The train was full, so I stood with many others and steadied myself by holding on to an overhead loop type handle. It was for me an amazing ride underground with noises of turning and shifting cars and a series of stations for brief stops to pick up or drop off riders. Stations were announced just before pulling in and I also could read the names on the wall at each one. There was a poster in the train that listed the route of that train and each of the stations were listed in order. As I looked around the train compartment there were many people of all ages including an elderly man with two canes and a woman with a small baby. Some riders were dressed in business suits with nice clothes including shirt and tie. Others were much more casual in attire especially a bunch of apparent students with back packs and books. I noticed several people talking to each other but in languages that I did not understand. The train car was truly a mixed collection of humanity all wedged into a small moving space. I could not tell how many cars were in that train, but I did realize that my little spot was small in comparison to the whole train. I vividly recall one young woman who was maybe 18-25 years old, dressed in jeans with a light-colored long sleeve shirt and dark long blond hair. In her mouth, she had a baby pacifier or so-called baby plug. I recognized what that was in her mouth and was surprised and somewhat mystified at the way she held onto a loop handle over her head yet continually sucked on that pacifier. I was jolted out of my people watching by the announcement that the next stop was Symphony Station. I made my way in a small group out the doors and onto a large platform with many individuals moving in different directions. I was no longer clear as to my next step, so I asked a few of the hurrying people and found a young man who insisted he knew how to get to the Brigham Hospital. I believe he directed me to a different level of the station to find the train to Brigham Circle and I got on that train. This train was more like a series of streetcars than a high-speed metal train. It was underground for a while and then came up onto the surface on tracks. There was a college on the left with many students gathering. Soon the train passed in front of what I later learned was the Boston Museum of Art, a formidable building that was set back from the street. In the front of that building was a huge statue of an American Indian brave on a horse with his arms partly raised up towards the heavens ,seemingly beseeching his gods for help. I was really impressed with that statue, and I believe a part of me could relate to that whole idea at the time. I ended up spending six years in Boston and every time I saw that statue I would pause and study it, recalling what it meant to the Indian nations but also to Rich Whiting.

Soon after the train passed that museum and its statue, it arrived at Brigham Circle where Huntington Avenue joined Francis Street at a small circle and that was at the actual entrance to the Peter Bent Brigham Hospital. Several of us on the train got off and headed toward the hospital. I went in the front door after climbing several steps and inside found the lobby where I was directed to a small meeting room. The new class of house officers was to gather there to start our day. Very soon we were greeted by the Chief Resident in Medicine, Dr Ting-Kai Li. He led us in introductions and some welcoming comments. As an aside, let me say that I suspect many who read this memoir will realize I was naive in that I actually thought my first day would be filled with learning the hospital itself and a lot of procedural guidelines. In actuality, the 13 "newbies" were given a brief tour of the hospital (Harvard grads really didn't need that !)so we could find our way around. This included our sleeping quarters (a true misnomer!), the emergency room, private patient wing, laboratories, radiology dept., and briefly down the pike toward the wards E2F2 and F main. This pike walk also passed the entrance to the Research Center. At some point we were split up and each pair of us taken to the location of our first rotation as house officers. Ralph Stoll and Rich Whiting were directed to the private wing and the second floor where the Levine Coronary Care Unit was located. It was in the general area of private medicine which included first and second floor of the A building and second floor of the B building. The Levine Unit had opened in March of 1965 and had been staffed by second year residents up to the time of our arrival. Ralph and I would be the first house officers to fill the roles of house officers in the unit. Since that highly specialized unit only had four beds, we would both also follow some private patients out on A2, many of which would have first come in by way of the unit itself and then progressed to need less complicated management.

Within minutes of arriving on the A pavilion, I was stopped by a second-year resident who was finishing his JAR year and knew that I was starting there as a new house officer. JAR stands for Junior Assistant Resident-basically a second year resident. In that same jargon, SAR was a Senior Assistant Resident or a third year trainee. My memory tells me that man was Dr Andrew Wechsler and he was friendly and professional as he started me on the road of house officership. He was basically passing the baton to me and happy to release it. Readers of this will probably realize this was a point of crashing my naivete that seemed like an ice bath as he handed me a list of the patients that I would be picking up and their room numbers and then handed me a small plastic box that hooked onto my belt. That was my first beeper. He told me that was my beeper, and I should keep it with me at all times since nearly all calls for me would come via that little box. He told me that if I hear it ring, I should then call the telephone operator and I would get a message. He then said "goodbye!" and "Good luck!" and was gone. Beepers like this one had only been introduced in the previous year at the Brigham by Dr Eugene Eppinger, the head of the residency program in medicine. It is my understanding that the really strong case for these beepers had come from the previous chief resident in medicine, Dr Marshall Wolf.

I can't recall how many names were on that first patient list but there probably were 8-12 of them so I knew I had to find these patients, read their charts, and introduce myself as soon as I could. I did have one piece of reassurance since I knew each of these patients had their own private physician who knew them fairly well. At about that time and before I could actually start to evaluate my new group of patients, one of the floor nurses on A2 asked if I was Dr Whiting. When I answered in the affirmative, she told me I should go to the Levine Unit for further information. OK, now can anyone reading this imagine how high my adrenalin level jumped? But just then-you guessed it-my new beeper went off. I called the operator and identified myself and so I was transferred to another line where a nurse I believe on the Renal unit wanted to know if she should continue to hold Mr. Somebody's quinidine. Quinidine is a very potent anti arrhythmic agent used a lot back in those days to treat or at times to prevent cardiac rhythm disturbances. I had experience with this drug in med school and was well aware of its possibility of inducing very serious side effects so I decided to ask the nurse to continue holding that drug until I could get there and review the chart. My personal "to do" list seemed to be growing into something like Mt Everest! I was already accustomed to making short notes for myself to organize all the little tasks needed on a given day.

The Levine Coronary Unit was very well equipped with state-of-the-art electronics including EKG and vital sign monitors. Each patient was monitored at their bedside with information about the EKG, blood pressure, heart rate, oxygen saturation of blood, and if needed other pressures such as venous pressure or in cases with an internal catheter in some part of the heart or blood vessels any pressure one wanted. In addition, all four patients in the LCU were continuously monitored on large slave scopes mounted at several places high on the wall of the unit thus allowing any and all personnel to see at a glance how each EKG looked and judge rhythm and rate.

The nurses in the LCU were truly unique. They all had critical care experience, and all had taken an advanced course in cardiac monitoring, physiology, arrhythmias, and pharmacology. That course included direct hands-on resuscitation of dogs in a fully equipped animal laboratory. That facility itself was unbelievable and located in the Harvard School of Public Health immediately next door to the Brigham Hospital. There was capability of humane care for the animals as well as detailed monitoring and lab support with full time research technicians. The head nurse of the LCU was MS B. J. Bonneyville and she greeted Ralph and I and proceeded to give us a tour of the entire unit. This included a review of the basic plans for care as well as several research protocols already underway. The main thrust of these studies and also of the care in general was to improve patient care, minimize the size of myocardial damage, and especially control or prevention of life-threatening rhythm disturbances. As an aside, I would say this kind of work had very significant impact on the entire field of coronary care .

The attending physician of the LCU was also its director, Dr Bernard Lown. He was very highly regarded in cardiology and also had shared the Nobel Peace Prize with Dr Chazof of the former Soviet Union for work to unite physicians against nuclear war.. Dr

Lown was also the developer of the cardioverter which could deliver a graded and specifically timed electrical discharge to the heart in order to terminate many abnormal cardiac rhythms. Once the cardioverter stopped a given abnormal rhythm, the normal rhythm nearly always returned. This device as well as the defibrillators that were designed to reverse ventricular fibrillation and some other very serious rhythm disturbances were part of the equipment at all med centers, emergency rooms, procedure rooms, surgical suites, and part of EMT vehicles all over the world because they were so crucial in very many life-threatening situations. Dr Lown and his lab had done a large volume of research in the use of defibrillators as well as the cardioverter. Dr Lown was assisted in directing the unit and attending physician responsibilities by his fellows in training and several junior associates. I recall the Fellows at that time were Dr Mike Rossi and Dr Stephen Wittenberg who both proved to be very helpful to Ralph and me on many occasions.

Ralph and I each had responsibilities in the LCU as well as outside on A2 and at times also on A main. During the daytime hours we both crossed paths off and on but at night only one of us was present on the rotation. We were both very obsessive about our patients which was surely true for all of the house officer group. In my particular case this meant studying the chart and then introducing myself to each of my assigned patients. On a daily basis I reviewed vital sign charts, nurses' notes, and any lab data that was new. I got into the habit early in my house officership of talking with the nurse who had actually been on duty the night before my review thinking they would be an excellent source of fresh information on my patients. As I discovered quickly, these nurses were very competent but also very willing to share their thoughts on care and potential problems. Occasionally, this interaction resulted in me learning something about my patient that while seemingly minor could be a significant clue to very significant problems. One such event that I recall was a man who had an unexplained episode of confusion in the very early hours of the morning. His vital sign chart did show a low-grade fever bump that was normal when rechecked. Thus there was some question whether this little fever was actually real. His apparent mild confusion cleared by the late morning and even he did not recall any problem during the previous night. The very next night, this man had a vague discomfort very low in the pelvic area and a temperature of 100 degrees. Further evaluation revealed acute prostatitis which was fairly easily managed. I remembered that my instructors from med school always harped on the need for an internist to pay attention to all details in evaluating a patient and this episode seemed to reinforce that thought.

I had acquired the habit in med school of carrying a small number of 3 by 5 cards to use as a sort of personal sketch of each patient I saw with details like history, outstanding exam findings, but especially lab results and x ray findings. I still had that habit and carried a small collection of these cards in one pocket of the short white coat that was common attire at the time. I became aware that my colleague David Livingston also used this same system to keep track of patient encounters. To complete the tools that I had with me all the time there was a worn copy of the Washington University Manual of Medical Therapeutics which was much like a "bible" for many residents all over the US and was updated every year, so it was up to date. This little book provided a succinct but highly pertinent review of a very large amount of medical information with special emphasis on medical care and medications. I know many of us in that era used this small document and it could really help to outline a condition that one had heard about but never actually seen. A great example that comes to mind was the information about myasthenia gravis so that, presented with a given patient with this entity whose symptoms were much worse ,the reader could quickly refresh the disease itself, and then review the drugs to make it better or worse. This kind of useful information could take a long time to look up in any standard text and of course no one could carry around books of possible need. This was before the days of the internet.

The last pocket in my white coat was filled with my ophthalmoscope-otoscope since we all did fairly comprehensive physical examinations at that time. Later in this memoir, I will describe how the otoscope really came in handy in ways for which it was never intended.

The first day in the hospital and that first night were constantly busy but not at a panic level. I even ate a ham sandwich that my wife had made for me, and I could read the patient charts at the same time. That night at about 11:30 one of the junior residents reminded me about the snacks available in the cafeteria at midnight. Out of a combination of hunger and curiosity, I did get to that snack session where the fare was fairly spartan: bread, peanut butter, jelly, fruit, coffee, tea, and soda (what Bostonians called "pop"). A group of residents came and went and as I recall there was even some complaining about the food provided. All of these men were well aware there would be no better food for them for a while and very likely little or no sleep, so they actively took part-possibly just for a short break.

I returned to the unit and resumed reading those charts and then started making my "to do" list for the next day. At some point in the early morning, I was feeling tired. My patients were asleep and there was a seemingly brief pause in the action. The monitors of course beamed out in the silence. One of the nurses told me it was OK and often done at such times for me to take a nap. So I did go to bed for a short time and asked the telephone operator to call me at 5:30 AM. Even though it was a short nap, it did seem to help, and I got up washed my face and shaved. I ate an apple and potato chips left over in my lunch bag and went back to the unit to catch up for morning work rounds. As I recall, there were regular work rounds on A2 for the patients Ralph and I had there and that was with the JAR on private medicine. Then we went into the LCU for work rounds with the cardiac fellow. Part of the review in the unit included all the rhythm strips collected showing EKGs during the night. As always, we both spoke with the nurses that had been with our patients and looked at the vital sign sheets.

On rounds that first day in the LCU Dr Lown discussed the management of acute coronary heart disease, heart failure, arrhythmias, and he also talked about an appropriate diet for anyone with actual or potential risk for atherosclerosis. The obvious example would be patients with hypercholesterolemia. Much of his discussion was right at the bedside and I noticed that the patient was very often the most attentive person in the audience. I learned that this was deliberate on Dr Lown's part because it added so much to patient care. The patients would learn some things but would also get a real understanding of resident and student education. The overall result was a certain comfort or relaxation on the part of a person who deep down inside was always worried in some way. Also on that first day on rounds with Dr Lown as on every such activity, he demonstrated parts of the physical examination and commented on its importance. He really stressed the need for meticulous attention to detail in history as well as examinations. Even thoughtful review of something as basic as vital signs was important. The easiest way to understand meticulous management was to point by point check heart rate, blood pressure, respiratory rate, oxygen saturation, body temperature, etc. and judge if any of that seemed inappropriate for a normal human at rest. For example, a patient quietly in bed resting who also had a pulse rate of 110/ min should raise at least a degree of concern. And so on through all subsequent findings on the exam. During the first week and also during these bedside rounds, a middle-aged man was admitted with acute anterior myocardial infarction. Dr Lown demonstrated for me and all the rest of the team on rounds how it is possible to palpate with one's hand the abnormal movement of the front of the patient's heart during the examination. By turning the patient slightly to the left and placing one's hand directly over the heart impulse it was obvious that instead of pulling away from the chest wall as it pumped blood out, the heart actually bulged partially outward thus pushing against the examiner's hand. Once I learned how to search for this finding, I became better at finding such dyskinesias and it became part of my regular exam for my whole career. In later years, I had the definite pleasure of teaching that technique to many other students and medical residents.

There was a brief episode that occurred at the bedside that first week that I recall. Several of us were gathered around the patient's bed as the history was being presented. One of the group leaned forward and placed his foot up on the lower part of the bed frame. Dr Lown stopped the discussion and turned toward the man with his foot on the bed frame and addressed his comments to all of us . He said it was not appropriate for anyone to in any way usurp the patient's space. He said we must have awareness of each patient's individuality and privacy and not encroach on that without strong reason.

That first week in the unit was so stimulating in multiple ways that it showed when I would arrive home. Johnny could see that I was tired but still seemed excited in some way. Some of that spilled over into our relationship as I was overjoyed to see her after being away most of two days under stress. I really felt a need for her tenderness I think even more than on similar periods as a med student. I need not mention to many who read this that my daughter Anne was pure joy and every day with an 8-month-old child is a wonderful new experience.

Sometime in the early part of my LCU experience, I learned firsthand what I had picked up from Dr Lown's fellows, that he could be a very demanding boss. This lesson for me started on one of my call nights in the unit at about 10 PM with a fresh admission. The patient was a 61-year-old man with a very clear history of the acute onset of severe, heavy type chest discomfort accompanied by shortness of breath, sweating, and a lot of apprehension. In the emergency ward the EKG showed fairly typical changes of a fresh anterior wall myocardial infarction. He was put on oxygen, an IV was inserted and he was given a small dose of IV morphine. He also received a single sublingual tablet of nitroglycerin. He did improve in the sense he had less pain and a definite decrease in anxiety and so he was sent to the Levine Unit and to me. In the unit the nurses and I welcomed this man and helped transfer him to bed off the gurney. He was placed on nasal oxygen, and monitoring was initiated including a finger unit for monitoring his blood oxygen saturation which was fine.

As soon as the patient was settled and monitoring in place , I completed a brief introduction and explained my need to ask some questions and do an examination and he was agreeable. As soon as I had completed my history and barely started on the physical exam, I noticed he seemed to change his demeanor and he was less attentive to me. The EKG monitor at the bedside alarmed and I could see a rapid, regular, wide complex rhythm that looked like ventricular tachycardia. That is a very serious rhythm disturbance with the starting point in one of the ventricles so the qrs is wide. Since it is fast, there is limited time to fill the heart before its next beat and since the ventricles are now autonomous, they are not pre filled by contraction of the upper chambers Therefore , there is commonly a marked fall of the actual amount of blood being pumped to the body including the heart itself. This rhythm is life threatening and needs prompt reversal especially in the setting of a partially or totally blocked coronary artery. A rapid heart rate means a dramatic increase in the need for blood and oxygen to the heart muscle itself. I recognized the change in rhythm and considered whether I should inject this man with a medication to reverse the rapid rhythm or to go directly to use of cardioversion with an electric shock to reverse his rhythm problem. I said something to him that I needed to put his bed flat and that he would be fine soon, but before I could do anything else, one of the nurses pushed the cart with cardioverter-defibrillator next to the bed, and a second nurse charged it, paddles were placed on the patients chest and the instrument was fired. He did jerk slightly, and the monitor returned to normal sinus rhythm. I saw he was recovering, and I tried to reassure him that he had developed a change in heart rhythm that was now fixed. The nurses put lidocaine into a bottle of IV fluid and connected it to the patient's IV adjusting the rate of delivery to provide a low steady dose of that drug in an effort to prevent repeat ventricular arrhythmias. Once such a problem has happened, there continues for a while to be a risk of recurrence, so it was common practice then to initiate a lidocaine infusion. That very often worked. The patient remained in normal rhythm and soon I completed my examination. I think I gave him a mild sedative and he did sleep fine while I sat at the foot of his bed and wrote my admission note and progress note. Of course, all that we had done I had to write as medical orders too. Soon the nurse told me Dr Lown's fellow was on the phone for me. That was a routine in the unit so any untoward episode would be reported to the fellow on call and then discussed with the resident who was present as well as the nurses. After I described all that had happened and the fact that the patient was in normal rhythm sleeping and seemed comfortable with good heart rate, blood pressure, and oxygen saturation the fellow told me he would come in early but not right at that time. The rest of the night was quiet, but I remained in the unit.

I got through morning work rounds and reviewed all of my patient charts and vitals. Soon it was time for attending rounds with Dr Lown. I recall feeling pretty good. There had been a serious problem but with the help of trained nurses even as a new house officer I had gotten through it and the correct things were done so the patient was looking fine. As usual, a crowd gathered for attending rounds including Dr Lown and his fellows, my partner, Ralph, our junior resident, several med students, and a few nurses. Nurses were not only welcomed at these rounds but actually encouraged to take an active role especially if they had been involved in any of the management of a given patient. That was another part of the rounding process that I agreed with -keeping the nurses involved and welcoming them at the bedside. In all my future bedside teaching, I encouraged the nurses involved to have some input. I had the impression that when the patient was being presented and discussed, he or she would take definite notice if their nurse was clearly a member of the team. So on this day we went to the bedside of my patient admitted the night before so I could introduce him to Dr Lown and present the history and findings. Dr Lown then asked the patient if he could do some of the examination and discuss the findings and of course the patient agreed. After his examination, Dr Lown reassured the patient and thanked him for his willingness to be presented to the group. He then led all of us away from the bedside to a side area for further discussion. Dr Lown then took the mounted rhythm strips showing the abrupt change from normal rhythm to ventricular tachycardia and then the return of normal rhythm with the discharge of the cardioverter-defibrillator. He paid special attention to how long it took before the shock was administered to correct this patient's rhythm. While I had thought we corrected that problem promptly, Dr Lown seemed unsatisfied. He counted out the seconds and my guess now was it probably was 45 seconds total and he launched into a discussion of how the heart already damaged due to shortage of blood flow and oxygen, still had to endure a period of no blood flow at all together with a rapid heart rate that would increase the actual need for oxygen . Thus, the infarcted or damaged myocardium would be enlarged. All of the negative side effects of any heart attack were known to be worse based on increased size of the area damaged. So, I passed from feeling mild exhilaration and confidence into a feeling of some kind of inadequacy. I don't think I was fully concentrating on the rest of those rounds that day.

At the end of that day, I finally arrived home where Johnny and little Anne greeted me at the door. In some ways I really needed that and even looking back now I realize I was so lucky to have that support at that time in my training. I told Johnny about my duty activities and especially the big case itself. She of course knew me well and picked up on what I had felt at the time of rounds with a sort of high becoming a low . However, she being very supportive took the approach that after all the patient was fine and in fact his life-threatening event had been resolved. I can't determine if her reaction was purely wifely support or whether in fact, she thought I was doing better than I felt. We had already been through several somewhat similar situations before during my time as a student. And then there was little Anne who was nothing but fun. No judgements, no complaints just a soft warm bundle of joy making baby noises. Like nearly every return home after being away there was time for holding each other and exchanging ideas of what the previous time of separation was like. There was supper and once Anne was in bed, for Johnny and I to just be close and she was always affectionate. I also routinely finished my evening with a review of my notes on the patients, looking up some things in the few books we had brought with us, and planning the next day's work. I can say once more, it would have been better if I had the internet available to fill in some of the data base on myriads of problems.

As a few days passed, I did feel like I was getting better at getting the work done and handling the ups and downs of acute coronary care. There were several protocols in place to guide my actions and the nurses in the LCU as well as those out on A2 were very helpful. I mentioned it before, but these women were very willing to help by filling me in on whatever had happened during my night away, I believe Ralph also learned to use this very rich source of patient information. Oh, the hours on duty and near constant stress did take a toll on both of us with a constant low level of general fatigue. My marvelous wife decided that it would be very nice if she and I could enjoy a really special dinner on the next Saturday that I was off duty. So, she wheeled Anne in the stroller to the local family type grocery store to get what she needed to make chicken cacciatore with salad, cooked vegetables, and home baked bread. She was excited about her plan and told me there would be a special dinner on Saturday night. I arrived home on that Saturday at about 11 AM after two long days at the Brigham and felt exhausted. Johnny could read that on my face as soon as I arrived home and we agreed that I should take a nap before dinner. I went down hard and slept soundly for 10 hours. On Sunday we did have the warmed-up meal she had planned, and it seemed to me the bulk of her disappointment was forgotten. In a broad sense, I have looked back on that episode and decided it was a prime example of the sacrifices made by spouses or significant others trying to support their loved ones in pursuit of a professional career or even military life.

Many of the patients I saw in those days were followed by Dr Lown together with his fellows, Mike Rossi and Steve Wittenberg. There were several others who regularly attended rounds in the unit and at times actually took over to lead them when Dr Lown was otherwise involved. One of these physicians was Dr William Hood, a well-recognized research cardiac scientist and an excellent teacher. He had already done a lot of good research on the effects of ischemic heart disease and was very knowledgeable in that area. Later in my training, I was fortunate to work with this man in the animal lab resulting in a few published papers. Dr Hood was a full-fledged clinician and was in an out of the unit a lot because of high interest in rhythm management. I remember one quotation from this man that puts a lot of acute care in an intensive care setting into perspective. I will say that the clinical context of this quote is crucial and some level of the kind of thoughts that permeate one's mind when dealing with difficult, life-threatening problems on a regular basis. There was, one afternoon, the admission of an elderly man with evidence of a massive myocardial infarction on the anterior wall of his ventricle. This fellow was very sick with very poor output of blood due to weak cardiac pumping of blood resulting in low blood pressure and severe heart failure that resulted in congested lungs and poor exchange of oxygen and carbon dioxide-ie, very poor lung function. This patient had received oxygen and then been intubated to attempt to control respiratory function and clear fluid out of his lungs. He had been given IV diuretics to try to clear some of the excess fluid due to the failed heart function. We added low dose of IV cardiac stimulant and repeated the IV diuretic. This patient's lab data suggested he had previously been without significant renal impairment and his chemistries were not far off but the serum enzymes that reflect injury to heart muscle were very high which we knew was a bad prognostic sign. The patient had several brief runs of rapid ventricular tachycardia, but they did not respond

29

to IV lidocaine which very often worked in similar settings. Several of us tried to make this patient comfortable as well as solve the problems of severe cardiac dysfunction but he then went into ventricular fibrillation. That is usually a terminal rhythm as the individual muscle fibers of the ventricles contract in a chaotic fashion all out of sequence so the heart in effect becomes a jelly like quivering mass with no forward propulsion of blood. This of course means no blood or oxygen supply to all of the body, all organs, and the heart muscle itself. The application of a brief burst of electrical energy through the chest in the form of a defibrillator shock can reverse this rhythm problem. That is life saving and it explains many of the survivors of cardiac arrest if the involved patient can be managed quickly. In this particular case the defibrillator fired correctly but the rhythm reverted only for seconds and returned to the VF. We did external cardiac massage, administered a more potent antiarrhythmic agent (procaine amide), gave an IV dose of sodium bicarbonate to counteract acidosis that results from very poor blood flow, and repeated the defibrillation. Once again it transiently reversed the fibrillation . Continued efforts failed to help and after some time the decision was made to admit defeat and stop further resuscitative efforts. This is always a very difficult time especially for those who are relatively inexperienced but in truth all of us feel somewhat let down and disappointed. Dr Hood took two of us aside and talked a little about the entire episode reminding us that when so much of the heart is abruptly damaged it is not unusual for the patient to pass away. That was when he said : "If you can't keep them alive when they are alive, you certainly cannot keep them alive when they are dead".

Experiences like this one were uncommon and by far it was more common to deal with a patient with smaller amounts of heart muscle damaged. Patients in that group had considerably less problems like heart failure, low blood pressure, poor oxygenation and when they had a sudden rapid rhythm it was considered to be a primary rhythm problem rather than a change in rhythm because of profound other cardiac dysfunctions. These so-called primary episodes of ventricular tachycardia would be similar to the episode I already described on one of my early nights on duty, often reversible and even preventable usually by the use of IV lidocaine. The LCU had at that time a protocol in place to vigorously treat ventricular arrhythmias. Infarct patients who had frequent ventricular premature beats, pairs of such beats, beats from more than one site, brief runs of three or more in a row, runs of ventricular tachycardia, or even isolated ventricular beats that happened very early in the cardiac recovery cycle thus abutting on the tip of the T wave were all treated prophylactically with an IV drip of lidocaine. I have forgotten the numbers but after about a year of this protocol, the Lown group presented about a year's data in this protocol to the annual meeting of the New England Cardiovascular Society and showed not one example of primary VT or VF in something like 300 consecutive admissions. This was so different from other presentations that day, that IV lidocaine became widely used in a similar pattern all over the coronary care centers. I was there in the Unit during part of that study and also saw other examples after my LCU rotation so I as an individual felt strongly that that drug was at the least very useful. I also liked the fact later in my life that one could measure the blood level of the drug to be certain you had achieved a therapeutic level and not a potentially toxic one. Now I need not remind anyone there have been enormous changes in the understanding of mechanisms of arrhythmias but also it types of therapy. My little experience with acute coronary care was tremendously helpful for me and I look back with a mixture of gratitude and confidence.

The day finally approached when Ralph and I would rotate out of the LCU and take up duties out on the adjacent A2 with some patients also on A main and on the B2 wing. This area was basically for all general medical private patients but by reason of proximity to the LCU there were always some patients with cardiac ailments in addition to all other types of medical diseases.

CHAPTER TWO: General Private Medicine

Our change in rotation from the LCU and private medicine, largely on A2 was fairly smooth and aided by the immediate proximity of the work areas. In addition, Ralph and I already knew several patients who had been in the unit and moved to a lower level of care. We also knew some of the nurses on A2 as we had worked with them for several weeks.

The type of patients we now saw were mixed in diagnostic categories although as above, somewhat weighted towards cardiovascular problems. In general, there was a lesser degree of severity too. Common cardiovascular problems on private medicine included for example people with new or poorly controlled hypertension, evidence of some heart failure, and chronic forms of coronary heart disease like angina, previous heart attacks, and arrhythmias or palpitations. In addition, we saw patients with all forms of medical disease including neurologic, renal, rheumatologic, infectious, pulmonary, hematologic, etc. The daily schedule for house officers was fairly similar to what we already had experienced: arrive early or start early if you had been there all night ,with chart review, vital sign review, and a brief check with the nurses from the night before. Check your patients and get prepared for work rounds with the JAR on private medicine so he could head off to morning report and talk about the new admissions or new problems. Try to get started on the work of the day, at times interrupted by new admissions. Attending rounds on the floor I think were Monday, Wednesday, and Friday with a group of clinicians, faculty members, and some researchers taking the role of attending for a block of time and thus exposing us to a wide variety of teachers.

As I recall, it was at about this time that Ralph and I started trying to go to Grand Rounds held once each week in the main amphitheater with a special guest speaker. These sessions were always packed and so often we stood in the back or sat on the floor. They were usually outstanding and very often featured a speaker well known from the Harvard Med School, or one of the other well-known institutions in the Boston area who presented a discussion of something in their field of interest in great detail. The list of Grand Rounds Speakers was a list of who is who in medicine.

Very often Grand Rounds would begin by presentation of an actual case and so one of the house officers or another resident or fellow would provide the details of a case that was pertinent to the topic of the day. For whatever reason, one of those early Grand Rounds that I remember was given by Dr Samuel A. Levine and it sticks in my memory. He was very highly regarded in cardiology after a long and productive life with graduation from Harvard Med School and then being an early house officer at the Peter Bent Brigham. He was primarily a private physician and had very many patients from far and wide. In short, he was revered at the Brigham and by the time of this Grand Rounds was well known around the cardiology world. There was some sort of folklore circulating at the Brigham during my days that dealt with this man-more later.

The actual topic for Grand Rounds that day as I recall was for this man to describe the use of physical exam tricks to help examine a patient with particular emphasis on the carotid artery reflex to slow down a patient's heart rate . Slowing the heart rate would allow more careful listening to individual heart sounds. He did review some of the known reflexes involving the nervous system and cardiac function and finished his long discussion by describing how he as a very experienced examiner discovered a small trick to diagnose true chest discomfort due to inadequate coronary blood supply (angina) as being separate from many other types of chest discomfort. That was a very common differential faced at that time for many physicians. As he described it, he learned that once he knew a given patient had two functional carotid arteries in the neck without evident blockage he would explain to the patient that he wanted to listen to the heart and at the same time gently push on first one side and then a little later on the other side of the patients' neck. Then with stethoscope in place over the chest, he did just that with gentle pressure at first very brief like simply on and off. When that yielded no change in the heart rate, he then advanced to pressure for a count of 1,2,3 seconds first on one side and then on the other. If no change was found with decreased heart rate, he might proceed to a five second try but that was usually not needed. Pressure on the carotid can result in a brief and definite slowing of the heart rate. As above,

33

this could improve the ability to hear the individual heart sounds. However, Dr Levine described that on several occasions he was seeing a patient during their chest discomfort. When he induced a decrease in heart rate, he knew that for a brief time the heart need for blood flow and oxygen was lowered simply by decrease rate as well as some minor decrease of vigor of contraction, and often by slight decrease in blood pressure. So, when he noted a definite decrease in the patient's heart rate he would say" Did that pressure on the side of your neck make the pain worse?" Dr Levine said many patients really want to please the doctor in some way and if they seemed startled and indicated, no the pain got better, he then knew he was dealing with coronary artery insufficiency. Readers of today have to keep in mind this was more than fifty years ago when detailed physical examination was the primary tool for a well-intentioned and caring physician. I believe that since I had been trained in that same concept at St Louis U. this really resonated with me and that is why after all these years it still sticks in my memory.

The day-to-day care on the private service was less stressful than the LCU experience, although there were still long hours involved and a certain level of stress at times. By this time Johnny and I realized the continued use of the MTA to go back and forth to the Brigham was ridiculous and horribly time consuming. We started looking at ads for cars for sale and I proceeded to select one. This turned out to be good evidence that I did not know how to shop for a used car. I did pick a nice-looking vehicle and one that was destined to become something of a classic. It was a 1955 green and white Ford Victoria hardtop. I very soon discovered what a terrible choice I had made in buying this car as it put out very black exhaust as evidence of burning oil and the oil gauge showed low levels, so I had to periodically add oil. The real problem with the car however was that it would die at every stop unless I put it into neutral and gently pushed the accelerator while it was stopped. Sometimes it was necessary for me to restart the engine. As I recall, I used that car for about six weeks and hated every minute of it. We talked it over and somehow managed to go ahead and buy a brand-new green Volkswagen beetle. As I look back on that activity, I still wonder how did we afford that? I have no idea, but I always wondered if Johnny got some help from her parents. That little car was really great for us both. I drove it to work often, but on occasions would leave it home and go on the MTA so Johnny could use the car. She and a neighbor lady would take the kids to places for picnics and similar trips. Before I leave this topic of automobiles, I need to describe another embarrassment. The VW dealer would not accept the Ford at all, so I was forced to sell it. Our street did not allow cars parking on the street and so we had little room for the older car, plus we really could not afford to pay insurance on two vehicles. It took one or two weeks, but I did get rid of that heap. The bad part was that I ended up paying a man $20 to haul it away. I do recall at least one nice effect of having that VW. One of the days that I left it home, Johnny and Anne drove to the Brigham with a picnic lunch for me. I got Ralph to cover for me while my little family group visited and ate together on the lawn between the Pike and the A building. This is a good place to add a comment about how all of us as house officers did from time to time get our partner to cross cover our patients for a short time. One of the really amazing examples of that was when David Livingston asked Bill Grossman to cover his patients on F Main at a time when Bill was on duty on the Research Center. He gave Bill his patient 3 by 5 cards and left for I guess about 2 hours. When David returned, he told Bill his wife had just given birth at the nearby Boston Lying In Hospital and presented Bill with a cigar!

Patients admitted to the private medicine service were quite variable with respect to complaints and problems. Examples would include a few people admitted with fever. Some of these would present with a recognized infection as the likely source of elevated temperature while others the fever was cryptic with no clear cause at the time of admission. Of course, there were patients admitted because of some type of pain and there were regularly admissions with some kind of gastrointestinal ailment like nausea, vomiting, diarrhea, or bleeding from the upper or lower GI tract. I think there were problems involving every organ system that presented in a jumble of different complaints. As I mentioned above, because of the proximity to the coronary care unit there was an increased emphasis on admissions with cardiovascular problems. Any resident physician or former resident can easily recall the time needed to write up a full and detailed history and physical exam together with a projected possible diagnosis and plan for evaluation and treatment that was required for each patient. Then there were daily and often multiple per day progress notes or procedure notes for every patient. This kind of documentation took time and was interspersed with new problems, interruptions, and various rounds. Therefore, it was very common I think for all of us to be sometimes late leaving the hospital even on a night off.

All medical centers with a reputation for high quality health care, or well-known active research, or simply lots of publicity become magnets for very wealthy patients and also for various celebrities from the entertainment world, industry, politics, sports, or similar pursuits. There are times when this form of patient referral reaches well across international borders. I personally never had the opportunity to deal with such a celebrity although later in my fellowship I had the pleasure of meeting and caring for a lady who had just left Iran where she had been special secretary to the Shah of Iran before he was ousted. One of my co -house officers, Dr Art Kales, did have a special encounter with a very notable patient. Art was the house officer on private medicine at a time when King Saud of Saudi Arabia was admitted to the medicine service. Art never talked much about the experience but some of our colleagues said the experience was of course very cordial and very professional. The King did well and was discharged. I learned much later of one interesting part of the visit to the Brigham by King Saud. While he was in his private room one evening, there was a small fire in a near-by utility room. Really not much fire but a lot of smoke and that made it out into the hallway so as a safety precaution, patients in the general area were escorted a distance away. Well, Art went to the King's room and explained the need to move down the hall and escorted the King and one or two attendants the short distance away from the smoke. As one would expect, the fire was settled, and the smoke cleared and there really was never any real danger to patients or staff. Everyone was back in their own rooms without further problem. However, when the day came for King Saud to be discharged, he presented Art Kales a very nice watch as a thank you and it seemed to Art that somehow, he was being thanked for saving the King's life!

In the fall of 1965 and during my rotation on private medicine there was another somewhat noteworthy admission to the Brigham. A woman was admitted who was said to be The Gypsy Queen. I first became aware of a huge change when I arrived early in the morning to start my duty hours and discovered the entire eastern side of the hospital entrance was covered by tents and automobiles. This large encampment on the front of the hospital created some congestion but a lot of discussion that day. I heard a tale about some kind of altercation between one of the junior faculty at the Brigham and a man who claimed to be the son of the queen. There had been according to the story, angry words and some kind of threat if the queen did not get well. I pass this along as an example of the kind of rumor mongering sometimes with facts and often with exaggeration that can occur in a specialized setting like a hospital when there is a significant event with little or no clear facts. In any case, the entire entourage of tents, people, cars, etc. cleared out within a few days and I understand the queen and her family were satisfied.

Much of the daily experiences on the private service are just as fuzzy in my mind as other rotations. I will outline a few of the encounters and experiences that do stand out in my memory. Like the previous rotation, I would arrive home after being on call one or two days feeling bone tired yet still keyed up from what had taken place in the hospital. In truth, these feelings were much worse later in my house officer year especially during periods of high patient acuity or dismal results of attempted care. I think some of those feelings while worse were at the same time tempered by their repetitive nature and seemingly getting accustomed to them. My wife was remarkable as she was so loving and tried to be so understanding even when I was on the edge of tears. She encouraged me to vent my feelings, but I soon realized some of what I told her was hard for her to understand and in fact hard for her to even hear. I started to filter the events I described to her in favor of events with happy endings or when possible, a little humor. Along this line there was one night when I came home and could tell her about a very unique circumstance that had a happy ending and it involved my partner, Ralph Stoll. On the afternoon near the end of my call night as I was writing progress notes and finishing up chart work, I heard the operator page over the loudspeaker: "Dr Stoll stat for A main, Dr

Stoll stat for A main!" I hurried to A main to see if I could help. At the bottom of the stairs leading from A 2 to A main there were several people gathered including two nurses, a med student, and Dr Ralph Stoll who was sitting up on the floor mildly confused. The actual event was gradually pieced together. I could see Ralph was not hurt and he seemed to be actually feeling pretty good. Apparently, he had been walking down the stairs heading to A main when he tripped and fell. He landed at the bottom and did get a good bump on the head. I thought he was stunned for a short time but in the meanwhile the nurse on A main heard the noise of his fall and looked to see what happened only to see a man lying on the floor at the bottom of the stairs and not moving. So, she ran to the phone and called the operator to call for stat help as was the custom in similar events. Since Dr Stoll was the Doctor of record, the operator called for his help stat. Within a short time, Ralph was sitting up and then standing and insisted that he was fine. Brief exams by two of us did seem to indicate that he was OK. From that event onward, I many times loved to tell the tale of my partner who was the only physician I ever worked with who was paged stat to his own code! So that night this was a good story for me to relate to Johnny and she asked about Ralph and finally smiled as she could see from my reaction that all was fine.

The next portion of this sequence of life as a house officer actually involved me as the patient! First, I need to provide a little background. On a Sunday off, Johnny had arranged for us to drive to the home of another couple also from the St Louis area who were in Boston for medical training. Dr William and Judy Hamilton were dear friends and Bill was studying cardiology with Dr Herb Levine. Judy was a registered nurse in St Louis but not active during the time in Boston. They each had a great sense of humor, especially Bill. For example, I recall a time when with a twinkle in his eye, Bill described life in Boston on our shoestring salaries. He told Johnny and I that their entire budget for any kind of entertainment consisted of an occasional bottle of beer and a used Playboy! He was correct, things were pretty tight for all of us at that time and that probably helps explain why Johnny and Judy would plan for all of us to get together for what we referred to as "communal dinners". Between all of us, there would be something like a potluck affair whenever our

38

respective call schedules would allow. We alternated which pair would host these fun get togethers for all the time that the Hamiltons were there in Boston. They returned to St Louis after a year as I recall.

On that particular Sunday at the Hamiltons, I discovered I had local tenderness at the tip of my right index finger. The area of greatest tenderness was just at the lateral junction of the nail and finger, so I recognized this was likely a paronychia. That is a usually bacterial infection just at or under the nail bed. I showed it to Bill, and he agreed. I think Judy had me soak the finger in a small glass of salt water for a while but there really was little else we could do at the time. We enjoyed our dinner and exchanged stories about life in Boston and in our respective training programs until time for Johnny and I to head home. Once we got home, I did wash the finger vigorously in hot soapy water but there was no sign of any drainage. I had to answer a series of wife type questions about there being no known trauma or bites involving the finger and then in classic male fashion I ignored the finger all the rest of that weekend night.

Monday morning, I was up early and off to the hospital which then led to immersion into the game of catch up to see patients, review charts, talk to nurses, and read over vital sheets. There also were two admissions for me that day so I was fairly busy. The finger still hurt, and it seemed more tender than the day before and by this time there was visible swelling and pink color just at the area next to the lateral edge of the nail. I showed the finger to my JAR, and he told me I needed to show it to Dr Eugene Eppinger who was the director of our residency program. He was well-liked, and I think actually admired by very many and affectionately known as "The Epp" by all the residents. Since my workload remained full, I put off visiting Dr Eppinger until the next morning after my call night. I think it was late in the morning when I presented myself to Dr Eppinger and by that time the fingertip was red, warm to the touch, tender, and clearly swollen. In addition, there was now a thin irregular reddish line running up my arm to the mid forearm. My temperature was noted to 101 degrees, but I really did not feel systemically sick. Before I realized it, the Chief Medical Resident, Dr Ting Kai Li was there, looked at the finger and was soon on the phone arranging for my admission to the hospital and for me to be seen by the surgical service. I was set up for admission to A 2 where I was actively assigned for duty. I heard plans for me to get blood work and some blood cultures obtained and then started on IV antibiotics. I understood my management would be under the control of Dr Li plus my own JAR and possibly my own partner, Ralph. Since this was the Tuesday after my night on call, all of my service patients would be under the watchful eyes of my partner Ralph together with our JAR. Another little twist to this tale was the fact that I had taken the car and driven to the Brigham at the start of my Monday on duty, so Johnny had no vehicle. I called her to tell her about all of these changes and tried to tell her that I was really quite fine, but she was very upset. She made some arrangements of her own by asking our cross the street neighbors for help. She arranged for Lucy Balian to take care of little Anne and Lucy's husband, John to drive her to the Brigham to see for herself what was happening to me. That was a brief visit, but it did serve to relieve her worries somewhat and I promised to call her later that night and again in the morning.

Things as planned moved quickly and I had blood drawn for testing and I think two sets of blood cultures. I was seen by members of the surgical residency and staff who examined me but mostly my finger and arm. I was started on IV antibiotics' and after several hours a transporter came with a gurney to take me to a small surgical procedure room. Under local anesthesia, the finger was incised, and a large drop of yellow fluid drained out. The wound was dressed in gauze and a small thin piece of gauze was left in the wound like a sort of wick. Fairly soon I was back in my room. As the local anesthesia wore off, I was somewhat surprised that the finger really was not that painful. Apparently, the release of that yellow fluid under some pressure resulted in overall decrease in the discomfort.

At this point I would like to comment on the nursing care. I have already indicated how impressed I was with all the help l received from many of the nurses on the LCU and A 2 floor with a definite feeling that they all really cared for each of their patients. Now, I could experience some of that caring for myself. I found myself feeling tired, a little hot, and very restless. I had made the call home and told Johnny that it was over, and I was fine. I just seemed restless and could not get to sleep even though I was tired from the day and especially the night before. The nurse came in the room to check my vital signs and replaced the bottle of IV fluids that had nearly run out. She could see I was not sleeping, and she asked if I would like a backrub. I had seen that done many times as a student and I understood it was part of nursing care. When I seemed a little reluctant, this woman indicated it would help me sleep especially if I did not want a sleeping pill. So, I agreed and that was a remarkable experience! She used a lotion and rubbed very hard into the muscles of my back and shoulders. It was sort of an amazing relaxation and afterward I did in fact get to sleep.

When morning came, I was awake and visited by several groups from both the medical and surgical staff. The finger was re-dressed and the wick removed I believe. I was of course given instructions on continued management of that finger and told that I would be switched to an oral antibiotic. In those days this kind of infection was nearly always staphylococcus organisms and back then they were often quite sensitive to penicillin and its antibiotic relatives. I was discharged with plans to return the next day for my regular shift and also told to report in so the wound could be inspected. I believe there was also a repeat visit to see one of the surgical team about one week later.

Over the months of the house officership, several of us had discussed how difficult it was to ever get time off. Part of that is understandable because being off meant your colleagues and especially your partner would get a definite surge in workload. We actually all joked about what it would take to get "The Epp" to grant someone a day off. We all knew of examples of various problems that once presented to him were not felt to justify time off. One of us had gone in to be seen with evidence of superficial thrombophlebitis in one leg and had been returned to duty. Then there was a junior resident who related a story about one of his group the year before as a house officer who did in fact get a short time off. All of us wondered how that was possible and the resident went on to tell us his friend had told Dr Eppinger that he was bone tired and that did not seem to be a giant concern . However, when he said he was losing his libido, he was given a day off! We all had a good laugh at that tale.

Before I leave this part of my memoirs dealing with my own admission there is a small tail end to the story. In the days that followed my admission, I of course mentioned to Johnny how much I appreciated that back rub. I guess I mentioned that too many times or maybe with a little too much feeling since she offered to give me a really good hard rub, starting with my neck!

There were several noteworthy episodes during this rotation on the private medicine service for me to relate and the next little story involves an example of house officership in action helping not only the patient but also the private physician. This was also a very easy story for me to tell my wife as it was not grisly, and it had a happy ending. It started one night when I was on call and had received several new patients. My usual habit was to quickly see each new patient so I could determine which order to really evaluate them so that those with some perceived urgency would be managed first. Of course there always was a tentative admitting diagnosis but in actual fact, my habit was to consider the listed diagnosis as something the patient did not have ,thus forcing me to get into my own differential diagnosis and not be influenced by the initial impression from a doctor's office or from the emergency room. One of my new admits that day was a 58-year-old lady with a severe headache. She had a well documented history of chronic hypertension difficult to control and she also had superimposed mild renal insufficiency. She had been given a small boost of her regular blood pressure meds and a small dose of demerol for pain control in the emergency room before admission to the floor. When I entered her room, she seemed relieved to see me but something about her really did not look good. She was still hypertensive with a pressure in the range of 165/95 and her pulse was steady but a little rapid. She admitted many previous headaches and several times they had been managed in our emergency room or her doctor's office. She insisted that this present headache was different from previous ones. It was very intense and located over the left side of the front of her head and orbital ridge. As I looked at her face and eyes, I was struck by the similarity of the image to an illustration I had seen in one of Frank Netter's books. Dr Netter was a physician who made a name for himself by providing excellent medical illustrations that were very realistic . His illustrations were widely noted for high quality and outstanding details. This lady's left eye looked cloudy, the white part was pink, and the pupil was slightly larger than the one on the right eye. The eye looked very much like the illustration for acute glaucoma! I told the patient it was very possible her problem was in the eye rather than the high blood pressure and I needed to speak with my resident and I would be right back. He and I came back and after a few questions and a brief exam, he agreed with my tentative diagnosis of acute glaucoma. He told me in front of the patient this was important, and I needed to call her private doctor immediately. I told the lady we would be continuing to follow her blood pressure, but I would be back as soon as possible. I believe I felt a need to tell her that it could be that she had some increase of pressure within her eye that would need care soon. I then went to the nursing station and called the operator asking her to look up the home phone number of this patient's physician and place the call for me. Once that call was made, I heard the voice of another woman on the line, so I introduced myself and explained that I needed to speak to the doctor right away. She indicated that she could not speak with her husband right then. I was confused and repeated how this call was urgent for one of the patients at the Brigham hospital. She then said something about being sorry, but they lived on 120 acres of ground and her husband was out somewhere riding his horse. So, I asked her to please have him call me at the Brigham as soon as possible. I wondered if I should wait a little or if I should try to reach the doctor who was on schedule to cross cover the one I needed. Before very long, I did get paged for a call and the doctor was on the line. Once I described the patient and her findings, he agreed this could be acute glaucoma and he would arrange for a rapid transfer of this lady to the Massachusetts Eye and Ear Hospital nearby. She was moved by ambulance, and I learned later that she did have glaucoma and was successfully operated thus saving her left eye. Once I learned that, I felt really good and knew I finally had a really good story to tell Johnny once I got off.

Approximately two weeks later, I was paged by the operator at the Brigham to tell me there was a package for me at the switchboard. Once I got free to go to the switchboard, I found a package with a bottle of wine and a thank you note from the patient's doctor. The wine was The Blue Nun, a lovely white

Liebfraumilch that was popular as a German wine for sipping. Johnny and I thoroughly enjoyed that bottle of wine which served to plant the idea in both of us that wine with dinner was enjoyable.

This gets me to early Fall of 1965, and I think all of us were feeling a little more secure in our activities and had regained our confidence that was strained a little in the first two months of rotations at the Brigham. I myself, did continue making notes about my patients and still tried to look up items that came up during routine rounds. My habit of going over my notes each night whether I was at home or at the hospital and then formulating some kind of a work schedule for the next day also continued. Since the patients themselves were changing and individual patient needs also changed, the " to do" list was constantly in a state of flux. Many items that appeared on my list were of course old friends in the sense that some of the same activities were required in multiple patient encounters. Examples would include starting IVs, drawing blood cultures, setting up x ray studies, and now and then a procedure such as a lumbar puncture. One fairly common item on the to "do list" for me was recording EKGs at night or after hours for the regular technicians. This gets me to another hard learned lesson that had to do with obtaining an EKG late at night. It seems, my junior resident reminded me about a new patient admitted because of an unexplained syncope or fainting spell who needed a second EKG after one done much earlier in the emergency room had been fairly normal. Basically, he reminded me that once in a while a random EKG could show a clue to the cause of a given patient's syncope spell. I already knew there were a few people who had very sensitive carotid reflexes and, in such people, even brief pressure on the area of the carotid artery in the neck could induce slowing or even a definite pause in their heartbeats. There had been a case described in which someone with sensitive carotid reflex had briefly lost consciousness by simply applying an electric shaver firmly against the side of their neck. Such cases are really rare, like merely turning one's head to the side while wearing a tight collar resulting in brief very slow pulse rate and light headedness. I was aware of these rare birds and at the same time I would love to be able to find the actual cause of someone's fainting spells, so I think those thoughts were briefly considered. In any case, a repeat EKG on the patient with unexplained fainting was on my to do list. As luck would have it, the workload for me that afternoon was very hectic, so I did not get to that part of my planned workload until much later. It was even past visiting hours in the hospital, but I still went to this patient's room and asked if I could record another EKG. He readily agreed and I probably said something about how there could be a clue on such a recording to help in his particular case. I set up the machine and recorded a complete standard tracing that looked normal to me. Before unhooking him from this recorder, I decided to go ahead and test him for any carotid sensitivity and asked his permission to press on his neck as I recorded some more of the EKG. He seemed a little skeptical but agreed. With the EKG machine running and making a recording that I could watch, I gently pressed on the right side of the neck right over the arterial pulse and nothing happened. So, then I repeated that but with gentle pressure for an estimated three seconds. There was slight decrease in the heart rate. That is not unusual at all. Then I went to the left side of the neck and again gently pressed on the pulse with no response and so then pressed on it for about three seconds. To my surprise, the machine kept recording but there were no more EKG complexes for ventricular beats but a series of smaller complexes from the electrical activation of the upper chambers of the heart-the atria. About the same time as my panic level jumped up, the tracing changed back to normal with all the expected waves. So, I realized I did discover a sensitive carotid reflex and fortunately the complete block of electric signals from the upper to lower chambers of the heart had been transient! I felt obligated to say something to this man and so I explained that the little test I had done did provide a possible clue to the cause of his fainting spell. I told him I would show it to my resident and be right back. I left the patient and quickly found my JAR and showed him the EKG. He reacted with shock and then launched into a major complaint that I had done this so late at night. There would be much fewer staff and colleagues around if this episode had been prolonged. I had little to say and finally he settled into admitting that right or wrong, I had in fact discovered a real possibility to explain the patient's syncope. As a matter of fact, the patient was seen by the cardiology group, moved to a monitored bed, and I am fairly sure that he received a ventricular pacer before discharge.

At about this time I finally met the person who served as the hospital barber, Gabriel. I think I had managed on a late Saturday off to find a barbershop near our home so I was not totally shaggy on the day I managed to get coverage for a haircut while at the Brigham. The main reason for me to include this part of life as a house officer it that Gabe as he was known really was part of the group of people supporting the Brigham in those days. The rumor was that Gabe provided haircuts for very many administrators, physicians, residents, and some students and he knew all kinds of things that were going on in the facility. Well, I did get a fast haircut but I did not learn any secrets that day or even on other haircut days.

Now I will pick up this story with a known date as on November 9, 1965, a very significant event in Boston as well as all over much of the eastern part of the United States and much of Canada occurred when there was a huge power outage. As I learned much later, at about 5:15 PM eastern time a series of electrical safety relays in a long chain of power stations began to shut down. I have no idea how this started, but once a relay closes that means electric flow stops in one path and that energy it diverted to another. If the diverted power is high enough it will trip the next relay and the long sequence of power interruptions progresses. At the Brigham hospital all power went out abruptly. There were limited areas with emergency generators like the emergency room, the operating room, some of the ICUs, etc. but the bulk of the hospital was pitch black. I believe there were small back up lights at many of the hospital corridor intersections that helped a little. There were flashlights in the drawers on every nursing station so that also helped a little. The hospital personnel were immediately drawn into fast action and into the solve problems mode especially in places like the operating room.

This particular day was my day off after being there all night. So, I was in the process of reviewing charts and checking on lab values just before the blackout and at the actual time I had just left the Radiology Department after going over the x-rays of my patients with the radiologist. Everything was black, so I reached into my coat pocket and pulled out my otoscope. This tool for examining the ear, nose, and throat was now pressed into service to show me the way in the dark. I easily made it back to A2 nursing station and joined in with others to check on the patients and try to reassure them as much as possible. Several people had called outside the hospital as the phones were still working and they indicated the blackout was not just at the hospital but all over Boston and in fact covered a much larger area. I think there was even some talk about this being some kind of attack on the United States. Over the next hour or two, there was no further change and nurses and others managed to keep everyone calm and the initial panic was somewhat abated. I also found a phone and called Johnny. She and Anne were ok, and she indicated the entire street was without lights. Mrs. Walsh from upstairs had sent down to her some candles and so she had some light. The Balians from across the street had come over to see if Johnny needed any help. So, it seemed my little family was OK. I told Johnny I needed to stay for a while to help but would drive home later and would let her know. I spent some time using my otoscope helping move patients from one place to another, like someone caught in a lab area or other office who needed help finding their way back to their bed. I was really not much help and so I called home and then left for the drive. There were no streetlights and no traffic lights, but cars all had headlights and people seemed fairly good at getting around and taking turns at intersections. Finally, I got home and got a very warm hug at the front door. Johnny made me a sandwich and I took a bath in lukewarm water by candlelight.

The next day was a lot like other mornings at the Brigham and it seemed everything was functional. At some point the power was restored. I learned much later that Newton Hyslop one of the SARs that year had similar experiences. He had just finished Radiology rounds with his team when the lights went off and went through trying to find his way back to his service and helping organize that area. Later, his wife drove in near to the hospital and picked him up as she also had a little apprehension maneuvering Boston streets without lights.

It is amazing how an event so monumental can be nearly forgotten in the daily chaos of a busy medical service. Within one or two days I was right back in my usual routine. There were daily new patients and one of them I remember was a very friendly and nice lady with diabetes, hypertension and a mild headache. She was really not a difficult problem and we actually hit it off immediately. She was on a better diet that had been reviewed in detail with her by the clinical nutritionist, her blood pressure had settled, and the headache was gone. She was to go home the next day and her son came to visit late in the afternoon. He asked to see her doctor, and then he told me his mother wanted him to bring me a present. He presented me with a thick, I believe double lined brown bag with two full sized lobsters. He was a fisherman in Gloucester and the lobsters were said to be fresh. I thanked him and also his mother and told her it was not necessary or expected to give a gift when one's care was completed. I had to scout out help from several people as to how I should keep these things as fresh as possible until later in the evening when I would take them home. I called my wife and told her what I was bringing home and that I had some ideas how to prepare them for our dinner late that night. She was as surprised as I was, and I could tell she had some level of apprehension about how to prepare the lobsters. She also told me that her little brother, Robert ,had been put on a plane by their parents and sent to Boston for a visit. He had taken a cab and was already at our home. Later that night, I learned that Johnny had gone upstairs to see Mrs. Walsh and had been given a crash course in lobster cooking. So, that night Rob and I ate two lobsters which were really a treat for each of us. Johnny decided not to try it and it took a while in Boston for her to also learn to enjoy such a special meal.

Interspersed between many of the above events were regular attending or teaching rounds. Any discussion of the attending physicians in those days really should start with our Chief of Medicine or as his official title listed him: The Hershey Professor of Physic and Medicine, Dr George W. Thorn. He was widely known and highly respected in medicine and especially in endocrinology. Many younger physicians and researchers had worked closely with Dr Thorn and done their research in laboratories under his guidance. Very often researchers as well as residents on elective and med students would all accompany Dr Thorn on his hospital rounds. I think there were occasions when one of his team of junior endocrinologists would conduct rounds for him when he was otherwise engaged. My memory tells me that I did not have Dr Thorn as my attending until later in the year, first on the Research

Center and then on the wards E2F2 and F main. I actually learned to really like this man. Folklore at the time indicated that he subscribed to over fifty medical journals and regularly read a lot of that material. One thing I do remember is that Dr Thorn sent a congratulatory card to Johnny and me at the time of the birth of our second child, Amy. That was early in my JAR year.

My first encounter with Dr Samuel A. Levine as an attending physician happened early in my rotation on the private service. I was paged and told to report to Dr Levine on A2. I arrived there and introduced myself to this older man fully dressed in suit and vest. He quickly shook my hand and then handed to me a patient chart. He then started dictating his admission note to me so I could write it in the patient's chart. I was a mixture of surprise, confusion, and at the same time some level of respect as I already knew who he was. Dr Levine was like the grand old man of cardiology and was revered by many. I already mentioned his Grand Rounds about carotid reflexes. He had graduated from Harvard Medical School in 1914 and then was one of the first house officers at the Peter Bent Brigham. He had very wide experience and I think he served also as an advisor to many notable people. There are photos of Dr Sam in the collection of memorabilia in the Countway Medical Library and one of them I recall showed a very young Dr Levine wheeling an elderly black man outside for some sunshine and fresh air during rounds. As time went on, I learned that Dr Levine and his then fellow, Dr Lown had taken a large step in medical care of coronary patients when they introduced the sitting up position for patient recovery. It seems odd now, but back in those early days it was thought that a person with a heart attack had to rest for long periods lying in bed. By sitting up the patients these men demonstrated that it was safe to move around and to be upright. In addition, the upright position was more conducive to easy breathing and a huge boost to patient morale. The days of prolonged bedrest at times requiring sedation and at times leading to serious complications were over. So, in effect, Dr Levine was even for an outsider like me, quite a figure.

He had a very noteworthy career and became fairly well known so that on at least one occasion he was invited to come to London to serve as a visiting cardiologist. At the time, the British physicians were very highly respected in all of physical examination with several men who were simply outstanding in cardiology and especially in listening to heart sounds. So, this man from America was invited but was also going to be questionably welcomed. The story goes that he was indeed presented a case for discussion in an amphitheater that was full. Dr Levine heard the presentation, met the patient and asked a few more questions. Then he indicated he wanted to listen to the patient's heart and bent over with stethoscope on the patient's chest and listened for a few minutes. He then stood up and faced the audience and started describing what he had heard. He described the first heart sound, a very soft systolic murmur, and the second heart sound in a little detail and then he paused briefly. At that moment, a whispered voice high in the theatre was heard to say, "He missed the diastolic murmur!". At that point, Dr Levine heard that whispered comment and said, "I have not listened to diastole yet". One of the things about the Brigham hospital is there are very many stories of this type circulating and many of them emphasize the primacy of the patient and the value of a detailed physical exam. These stories served to increase my interest in this man. Obviously, I was aware that the brand-new coronary care unit at the Brigham was named for this man. So, yes, I did take his dictation at the time. When I mentioned this episode to my JAR I learned that Dr Levine had been doing that kind of dictation for a long time and there had been some discussion that it was not really the job of the house officer to take dictation. I learned that several of the faculty at the time had wondered how to speak to Dr Levine and get him to stop that particular activity. A short time later, a plan was set into motion for one of his former students and a good friend to approach him on this subject. That was Dr Roe Wells, the director of Rheology or blood flow dynamics. Dr Levine apparently took the request seriously and stopped paging house officers to act as his scribes. He seemed to cut back on the number of patients in the hospital, but I still saw him from time to time. One day, I got the idea and also a little courage to ask Dr Levine if I could have a signed copy of one of his many reprints from his publications. He readily agreed and told me to drop by his office which was on the Pike. Later that day, I did get free for a time and so I found his office and went in the door. I was greeted by a woman who I assumed was his secretary. She heard my request and sent me into his office. He was cordial but seemed a little brusque. He told me to sit down, and he turned away from me leaning over his desk. I could see that he was writing on what looked like a journal reprint. He quickly turned toward me and handed me a thin set of paper and said, "Here you are, Whiting!" I thanked him and left the office without really looking at the reprint. Once I had gotten back to A main, I looked at the document. It was as I had requested a copy of one of his publications-only a few pages that dealt with how important face to face contact of physician to patient was in rapport as well as finding the correct diagnosis and management. As scientific publications go, this was low key, and I thought he could have given me much more meaningful material. Then I noticed that he had written a note on the front of the publication which said : "To be taken at HS instead of seconal". Was he being humble? Was he chiding me for being such an eager beaver? Was he simply having a little fun with me? I have pondered those type thoughts for all these years, but I did save that reprint. Dr Samuel A. Levine passed away only a few months later on March 31, 1966.

One attending physician that I had for only a brief time was Dr William P. Murphy who together with Dr. George Whipple and Dr. George Minot had shared the 1934 Nobel Prize for their work solving the causes and then the management of pernicious anemia. That is an uncommon entity now, but back then was a rather complex illness that resulted in anemia basically because of a defect in the absorption of vitamin B12 from the upper part of the GI tract. Dr Murphy was somewhat quiet and very pleasant but not very dynamic especially in comparison to the rest of the group of active attendings at the Brigham at the time.

One of the attendings that I had several times over my house officer year was Dr David Ulmer. I believe I first met Dr Ulmer on the private medicine service and then worked with him later in the year in the Clinical Research Center. He was a very patient observer and would listen carefully to the history and my exam but always did part of the physical exam himself. I thought that was his way to remind all of us at the bedside of the immense value of a detailed history and examination. My memory tells me sometimes these displays of exam skills were not really needed yet they were time consuming. Now as I write this memoir, medicine has passed shamefully into a new era with seriously compromised time for detailed history taking and examination. That very fact has already contributed to somewhat of a loss of those particular skills. Now, physicians are rushed through patient encounters and the lack of careful exam or history retrieval is quickly turned into ordering multiple tests. In my opinion, the detailed history and exam would in fact eliminate many of those tests simply because they would no longer be relevant. As I think back on Dr Ulmer, I recall that he always placed his hand on top of the patient's head and pushed downward. This would produce pressure on the upper cervical spine and might then reveal unexpected tenderness. I never encountered a patient in whom that maneuver produced some kind of discomfort and in fact that part of the exam was dropped from my usual routine. I have continued to believe as did Dr Ulmer that there should be no substitute for a careful and thoughtful gathering of a detailed history followed by a detailed physical exam. I wish there were more examples of this in the present medical world. I have gone so far as to write to the major medical organizations, like the American College of Physicians and a few magazines or other media urging that when they show someone examining a patient, there should never be an example or depiction showing the stethoscope on top of a shirt, blouse, sweater, or coat. That is the way a listener would examine the heart or lungs if he or she really did not wish to have to deal with hearing unexpected sounds. Clothing simply provides additional friction noise and drowns out nicely any other somewhat soft sounds. That one image of an exam with stethoscope over a filter has always really bothered me.

Many of the attending physicians at that time had very active and productive research labs or clinical facilities with a large amount of regular clinical studies such as a cardiac catheter lab. Dr Lewis Dexter and Dr Richard Gorlin each had busy catheter labs and each were well known in cardiology and they also served as attendings on the private and ward medicine services. I will discuss Dr Dexter a little later in this memoir but address Dr Gorlin now. It's fair to say with different catheter labs, different personalities in charge of them, and also non catheter type prominent cardiologists all at one institution there were at times some episodes of rivalry or tight competition. All of these groups of course had full time trainees or fellows in the process of providing care as they gathered experience and advanced training. Of the three cardiac leaders that I had as attending physicians, I would have to say Dr Bernard Lown was clearly the most dynamic bedside teacher. Still, it is very true that different mentors add enormously to one's clinical education and I remain grateful to all of these men as well as their fellows and chief fellows who contributed to the teaching of house officers at that time.

Dr Richard Gorlin was widely known in the cardiac literature with many publications and a lot of research. He was also known for his work on the Gorlin Formula which was an equation very widely used to accurately estimate the actual size of the aortic valve orifice and later applied somewhat to other valves. The function of a valve can be estimated by taking into consideration a host of features such as heart rate, pressure gradient across the valve, amount of actual blood flowing through the valve, the resistance to blood flow beyond that valve, whether the valve is not only narrowed but also regurgitates(or leaks), etc. To be able to accurately estimate or measure the actual size of a valve particularly when it is irregularly scarred is a huge benefit. That allows more accurate decisions concerning whether a given valve really needs to be repaired or replaced and it also tells the correct size to select for a valve to be replaced with best results. So particularly at the time frame of this memoir, the Gorlin formula was an important facet of catheterization medicine.

Dr Gorlin was one of the attending physicians at the Brigham and I don't think he went to any other hospital. He would therefore now and then see a patient on rounds that he had seen in the past. Some of these patients were in his own group and they would be very familiar to him. He used a system of brief diagrams to quickly outline a given patient's heart sounds so by looking at that diagram and especially if there was a previous one available one could easily see what kind of changes had occurred in the heart sounds. He would draw a straight horizontal baseline and then along its length put in marks to represent all the heart sounds. For example, the first heart sound or S1 would be depicted and also the second heart sound or S2. The second heart sound commonly has two components, one due to closure of aortic valve and one due to closure of the pulmonic valve. These would be marked as A2 and P2 respectively. Some times there would be other sounds like noises related to heart failure, or murmurs, or clicks, or actual rubbing noises. All of these various sounds were depicted in Dr Gorlin's little diagram. That way he could visualize the sound of a patient's heart and also compare it with any of his previous diagrams. I don't know where he got this idea, but he used it often and in fact I adopted the same system and used it for years. A diagram is after all ,much better than a long string of sentences, so it was of use to me, and I also used it in lectures to students and residents over the years.

The next commentary on one of my attendings shows one of the perks of having attending physicians who were unusually generous with their time, and I guess recalled their own period of training. It was at the time a sort of unwritten and also unexpected part of some attendings activities to invite the team that was involved in the attending rotation over to a local restaurant or even to their home at the end of that rotation. Along this line, I want to describe a spectacular example of this due to the generosity of Dr John P. Merrill. To be honest, my memory can't tell whether this episode was during my house officer year or possibly one year later as a JAR but it still is remarkable.

Dr Merrill was a member of the medical and surgical team that had performed the first successful kidney transplant and had done it at the Brigham in 1954. Other members of that team included: the surgeons Joseph E. Murray and J. Hartwell Harrison as well as George W. Thorn and Gustave Dammin. The Nobel Prize in Physiology was awarded for this work in 1990 and was accepted by Joseph E. Murray alone since by that time both John Merrill and J. Hartwell Harrison had died. Historical details of that acceptance indicate that Dr Murray gave appropriate credit to all the members of that team that had taken part in all the preparatory work as well as the actual transplant and the post operative management.

Attending rounds with Dr Merrill were a tour de force of metabolism, acid-base balance, and fluid mechanics. Every session with him was amazing in details and also at times completely new information. He was brilliant but very kind and easy to like. I understand he was involved in very many projects and full-time department responsibility, and he would at times wear a white coat when walking through the building which everyone knew meant he would rather not be disturbed at that time. He was for us an excellent teacher about some of the most complicated medical physiology.

At the end of that rotation with Dr Merrill, we all on the team including medical students I think were invited to his home for dinner. I believe I was actually off that night which made it better for me but the person who really enjoyed that night was Johnny, my wife. She was really delighted to get out one night, so we left Anne in the care of our neighbors across the street-John and Lucy Balian. When Johnny and I arrived at the Merrill home we were amazed as there was a lot of land, a large, impressive home, and even a carriage house off to one side. She and I agreed we would be happy to simply move into that carriage house! We and a few others were greeted at the front door and coats were taken. We were all directed into a large living room or sitting room and asked about drink preferences. As we settled in and there was a little small talk, we were taken to an adjacent very large flat room with canals of water running through it. One could walk around these canals and see in the water several fish. It soon was made clear to us that we could point out a trout and a man dressed like a chef would use a net and haul it out and take it to the kitchen. Well, that was then and still is now a simply unbelievable and fantastic experience! I realize there is no way each of us actually got the fully prepared trout at dinner that we had selected but that really did not matter at the time. The dinner was excellent and served with a really enjoyable white wine. There was a dessert and coffee time as I recall and then we went back to the sitting room for a while. I think that was when the host, Dr Merrill asked the men if they would like to see his basement and the facilities for keeping the fish in normal health. So, we did go downstairs, and he demonstrated a complicated set up of tanks, pipes, valves, and some kind of meters to tell temperature, pH, etc. I don't know how others felt, but I was totally overwhelmed. There were several other attendings who did something social for the teams that I was on, and all were appreciated, and all were of enormous generosity. However, the dinner at the Merrill home was clearly outstanding.

This is a good place to transition off private medicine rotation for me and Ralph. It was an amazing experience and the net effect for me at least was very positive. The next rotation would be quite different as it was on The Research Center.

CHAPTER THREE: The Research Center

Reporting to the Research Center was clearly different from previous rotation changes but this time I was much less anxious. I had completed the coronary care unit and the private medical service, both of which were vastly more intense than this present assignment. Each admission would be seen immediately on arrival in the Center for history and physical exam but very often the patient's arrival was preceded by their medical record. This meant I could get familiar with the patient's active problem for which they were being admitted and in addition all their previous history as well as lab studies. Some of these admissions were sick but usually not seriously or acutely sick. There were patients being evaluated because of hypertension, diabetes, weight control, thyroid disease, adrenal problems, bone metabolism, inflammatory bowel disease , lipid disorders, allergies, and many other afflictions. In every case , there was a researcher in charge of the patient and the study . That also meant there would be that researcher's trainees, residents on elective studies, and medical students involved in the patient's over all maintenance. I really enjoyed working with the med students. They were truly interested in learning and soaked up information like sponges, and very often were the source of very good questions.

The Research Center had opened in 1961 to provide a comprehensive area for research on a variety of disease entities. Brigham staff members both from the Medical and the Surgical sections were allowed to submit written detailed protocols for possible study. These proposals had to include the scope of the problem to be studied, detailed description of the methods to be used, and some projection of the likely value of the study relative to the targeted disease itself. A committee of hospital staff leaders would then review each submitted proposal and decide which if any deserved inclusion in the overall research protocols in use within the Research Center. Then there was a separate Advisory Committee that oversaw the actual studies and reported directly to the Hospital Director and the Dean of Harvard Medical School.

The Research Center had its own nursing staff and in addition its own Nutrition staff dedicated to providing all of the nutritional needs for each patient on the Center. Since patients on some of these protocols would stay in the Center for long times compared with general hospital admissions, there was an amazing educational program in place that was largely run by the nursing staff. This program served to educate the patients and at times their family members about the way their studies would be done and in general about their illness under study. There was also a program in place to provide a level of Occupational Therapy simply because so many patients would be in the Center for many days or even weeks. I think I helped with the educational program a fair amount, but I don't recall even seeing the occupational one in action.

The Research Center was funded largely by the National Institute of Health (NIH) There were several smaller support groups I believe and several of the researchers were also funded by the Howard Hughes Institute. Many of the senior researchers were Howard Hughes Research Fellows and Dr Thorn himself, the Chief of Medicine was such a Fellow. The rumor at that time was also that Dr Thorn was in fact Mr. Hughes private physician and from time-to-time Howard Hughes would pull into the Boston train yard in his private railroad car and Dr Thorn would drive there to see him as a patient.

The daily lab work was largely obtained by nursing and lab personnel, however at night this duty fell to the house officer. Commonly, urine or blood samples would be needed at specific times. For example, blood might be needed a few hours after a meal or the administration of some medication. Therefore, there were many examples of house officer obtaining studies at various times after regular hospital hours.

There were relatively few cardiac or renal patients on the Center simply because there were ICU's, the LCU, and the Renal transplant Unit elsewhere in the hospital. In all fairness, I should add that in fact most of the cardiac and renal admissions were of a more acute nature and not set up for research protocols.

The attending physicians in general were the actual study directors or their close associates. The reader can imagine with so many different types of problems under study, there was a true smorgasbord of teacher attendings for Ralph and me. In fact, I can't begin to describe many of them in detail although I felt like they each contributed to my overall medical education. I will mention a few of these clinical researchers and I have to rely on my memory plus a few comments from some of my house officer group. I indicated at the beginning of this memoir who in the group helped me and every bit was appreciated. Several of our group had passed away by the time I started working on this book and in fact one or two indicated they did not think their memory was as good as mine or that they simply were not totally well and did not wish to be involved. This same problem really bothered me all along as many of my mentors, friends, and SARs were not available to add to this memoir.

From an Endocrinology standpoint, George W. Thorn, David Lauler, George Cahill, and from the Boston Lying In Hospital, Kendall Emerson provided me a lot of bedside teaching and a lot to look up on my own. I believe Dr Herbert Selenkow had patients in the Center during my rotation to study thyroid disease and in particular Graves' Disease often with overactive thyroid gland leading to hyperthyroidism and in addition some had thyroid ophthalmoplegia. That was due to swelling of the soft tissues immediately behind each eye thus distorting the eye position within the orbit. That interfered with normal bi ocular vision and also could be a visible impairment as the eye on one or both sides could be displaced forward or at an odd angle. To this day, thyroid eye disease is still a definite problem.

Dr Frank Howard and his mentor, Dr Roger Hickler both were active with protocols dealing with hypertension. Some of these studied the effect of renin, aldosterone, and other hormonal type compounds. Some of these patients required blood work during the night or early morning.

There were several patients being evaluated due to severe hyperlipidemia. I had seen a few of these type people during my med school rotations including a really beautiful young blond woman who had lipid deposits on tendons of her hands and very high level of cholesterol. On the Center, there were several examples of the ravages of very high lipids such as premature atherosclerosis with prior myocardial infarct or severe muscle pain on walking called claudication .This was directly related to significant partial blockage of the arteries to the leg muscles in which exercise would increase the demand for blood and oxygen in the working tissues but the blocks in the arteries could not supply that increased need leading to a form of ischemia and thus the pain and muscle cramping. There were of course many patients with collections of lipids called xanthomas in tendons and connective tissue particularly the elbows, hands, and other joints but also involving the eye lids and the eye itself. Since those days, there have been enormous changes in the understanding and management of hyperlipidemias and of course several effective medications.

I believe there were a few patients that I saw who had reacted to some kind of IV infusion of x-ray contrast material to examine heart or blood vessels by going directly into anaphylaxis or allergic type shock. The protocol for such patients was designed to see if there were other allergies and then to see if tiny doses of the offending agent would be tolerated and if slowly increased over time would lead to the patient becoming tolerant to the drug.

There were several patients that I saw on the wards as well as a few on protocols in the Research Center who had inflammatory bowel disease, either Crohn's disease largely affecting the small intestine or ulcerative colitis that primarily damaged the large bowel. Some of these patients were truly miserable due to episodes of abdominal pain, bloating, diarrhea, intestinal bleeding as well as a variety of serious complications including perforation of the bowel and at times obstruction. Some of these patients had already had surgical removal of part of their intestinal tract to attempt to suppress their symptoms. At this time, I believe Dr Phil Snodgrass was director of the GI Division of Medicine and he was also the acting head of the Research Center.

I already mentioned that the Center had its own dedicated full time dietary service with clinical nutritionists able to provide any type of dietary material needed by the patients or needed because of the research. One example that I recall was the Giordano-Giovanetti Diet which was I believe originally formulated in Italy and was fairly new in 1965. This was a change in food type and amounts to result in low levels of protein, potassium, and phosphorous as part of a diet for those with renal impairment. The GG diet was used on the Center for chronic renal insufficiency patients but by this time it was commonly used also on the hospital wards.

Since the day-to-day workload for me was less intense and more organized, it meant that this particular rotation provided me a better opportunity to get home earlier on nights off. That translated into more time with Johnny and little Anne. She was changing so fast! Instead of me just hearing about all her new skills, I could actually see them myself. On weekends off, this rotation was good to provide Johnny and I a chance to catch up on some of the local history that we both felt was great. We lived in Arlington Heights which really was not far from The Concord Bridge and from Lexington Green both noteworthy sites from the very early fighting of the American reach for freedom from the King of England. I recall Johnny and I did have to ask directions a few times and we were somewhat surprised that local people did not seem familiar with either of these places. I came to believe that it is a sort of a truism that people who live in a given area are likely not to have experienced the very sites for which the area is known. As an example, I can cite St Louis and the fact that many St Louisans have not experienced a visit to the Arch Museum or gone up in the arch for fantastic views of the city and Mississippi River. As for Johnny and me ,we really liked finding our way to famous sites like Bunker Hill, the Old North Church, and we even drove to a cemetery called Sleepy Hollow ,said to be the locale of the story by Washington Irving about Ichabod Crane and the Headless Horseman. We drove there late in the afternoon when there were long shadows from trees, bushes, and of course from tombstones. There was a gentile breeze that moved the leaves slightly and we honestly felt oddly threatened. So we cut short that visit and didn't even get out of the car to read any of the stones.

This was also a time for me to catch up a little on my own neighborhood. The Balians were across the street and were marvelous neighbors. Johnny and I both loved the Walshes upstairs and she had been helped a lot in my frequent absences by both Lucy Balian and Mrs. Walsh. Tom Walsh was a quiet man and I really never got to know him well. The Walshes let me use the driveway and its attached one car garage simply because my hours were more unpredictable than Tom's. He did leave for work fairly early each weekday and was back home before me.

I wish to pass on a brief example of amazing reliance on us for our neighbors although it occurred right after my house officership when I was in my JAR year. We had welcomed our second child, Amy, into the family and were pleased that Anne really welcomed her too. On one of the days that I was at the Brigham, Amy climbed up out of her crib which was fixed with an extra low mattress, and she fell to the floor. The noise attracted Johnny in the next room and when she got to the baby, she was not responsive. Johnny scooped her up and ran over to the Balians for help. Amy did then start waking up, but John was late for work that day as he drove Johnny and Amy to Children's hospital while Lucy took care of her kids and Anne. The trip to the hospital resulted in an exam and some time away but in the end was fine and little Amy was OK. This story does serve to reaffirm how really wonderful our neighbors were in Boston and how very much we needed their support. It also of course tells a little of the usually unheralded hardships associated with young married couples, child rearing, and living far away from family.

Getting back to my memoir itself, there was another story worth telling concerning some of the events centering around our home in Arlington Heights while I was at my duty station at the Brigham Hospital. My wife was of course often alone with our little girl. As I mentioned already, she had developed a friendship with Lucy Balian just across the street. They shared morning coffee together and since the two houses basically faced each other, they could sort of look in from time to time. I know there was at least one time when Johnny looked across the street and noticed that the Balian kids were not quietly in bed but were up and about in their room. She called Lucy and let her know as they were that close. Then, one morning as Johnny got up, cleaned up Anne, and prepared the morning coffee, she looked across the street and saw a furry looking very small object or animal lying in the street where the driveway entered the street. As she studied that object she thought it looked like a small animal and it was not moving. She knew that our next-door neighbor had a cat, and it did wander the neighborhood. She also knew that Tom Walsh had already driven out to go to work. She thought: "What if Tom ran over that cat and didn't know it?" She couldn't be sure even if it was an animal, but it sure looked like it was and as I mentioned, it was not moving at all. Then she realized that the Balian kids would be up and then likely out in their yard so it could be awful for them to find a dead cat. That was an experience she did not want them to encounter so she called Lucy. After telling what she thought she saw and Lucy looked out her front window and agreed it probably was that cat and it was likely dead, the two of them panicked. John Balian was gone and so was I and neither of the ladies wanted to go out and pick up a dead and possibly bleeding cat and get it out of the kids view. After some discussion, they decided there was likely some kind of animal service or rescue they could call. So, Lucy looked in the telephone book and then started calling for help. She did find a group that told her they would send out a man with a small truck to pick up the dead cat. Lucy played with her kids and more or less kept them near the back of the house. Soon, a small truck pulled up and parked. Johnny alerted Lucy and they both started watching out their respective windows. A man got out of the truck, and they saw him walk up and down the street and even look on the other side of the street. He seemed disgusted. Finally, the two ladies went out on their porches and called out to this fellow. He asked if they had called for help to pick up a dead cat. Lucy admitted that she had made that call. The fellow looked at Lucy and said: "Lady that is not a dead cat! It's a stuffed toy dog!" Apologies poured out from both porches with no clear effect as this fellow drove off in disgust. Once John and I heard of this episode, we both had a good laugh. This little scene also became for me a common story to tell good friends and family over the years. Hidden in all the chagrin, was the clear fact that these two women had become close friends and also what it means to really live in a neighborhood.

The sum total of activities on the Research Center was time consuming but still basically low in stress. The time there passed fairly quickly and soon I was considering my next rotation. That would be much more difficult than The Center as it was on the female ward, E2F2. I did go briefly over to that ward to look over the physical setting. I was able to tell all my patients on the Center about the fact that I was to rotate to my next assignment and a new house officer would take my place. Writing the off-service notes was easy as I knew the patients well and there was plenty of time to write sensible   notes.

CHAPTER FOUR: Female Ward Service

I was really charged up to begin my first completely ward service. I knew I would have more responsibility and very likely there would be some very ill patients at times. On my first day on E2F2 I presented myself very early at the nursing station. I already had a list of the patients I would inherit from the previous house officer. I met the head nurse, Ms. Shandlin I believe and she in turn introduced me to several other nurses and showed me around the nursing station. I think she had been the head nurse on E2F2 for a few years and it became evident to me that she was highly regarded by nursing staff and also by the residents. A general medical service in a teaching hospital is heavy with problems to solve and there are often definite needs to organize workload, patient contact, and resources. Ms. Shandlin and her staff were really very efficient at making chaos turn to some kind of orderliness. At the time, there were very few male nurses and in fact many of the nurses were graduates of the Brigham Nursing school. In those days, it was customary for the nurses to wear not only pins on their collars that identified their school background, but also often the nursing school hat so it was possible to see directly how many of these women were trained within the Harvard system and often at which hospital. These women were experienced and professional which provided very helpful organization of day-to-day activity. Particularly the need for some procedure such as lumbar puncture, thoracentesis, emergency resuscitation, or events as simple as drawing blood cultures would all be smooth and when needed kept sterile by the direct assistance of these nurses.

On arrival at E2F2, I also met my new SAR who was in charge of the floor, Dr Newton Hyslop. I didn't know it then, but this man would soon become a hero for me and someone I admired and deeply appreciated. There were six Senior Assistant Residents (SARs) at the time. I really liked all of them but one or two I did not work with on a close basis. The three SARs that I did work with will be covered in this memoir: Newton E. Hyslop, Shaun Ruddy, and Nelson H. Perez-Trujillo. The other three were of course excellent in background and experience and my time with them was off and on but usually fairly brief. These three were: John H. Moxley III, Alfred F. Parisi, and Richard L. Tannen.

Newton Hyslop was a true New Englander and graduated from Harvard Medical School in 1961. He was deeply committed to infectious disease and would pursue advanced training in that field some time after serving as my SAR on the female ward service. Newton had just completed two years at the NIH as a Research Associate in Immunology. He was very knowledgeable but also patient with me. He would often guide me and at times provide definite critique, however, he also let me see the new patients on my own and perform a history and physical exam with the expectation that I would then formulate a reasonable plan for workup and initial care. Newton was an excellent role model and someone that I could easily learn from. In my off-duty hours, I recognized that he reminded me of a medical resident who mentored me during my Medicine rotation during my junior year at St Louis U. School of Medicine. That was Dr Al Grindon who was my resident back then and provided a lot of bedside and chalkboard teaching for the small group under his tutelage. He was also a forceful teacher and somewhat demanding as he assigned to all of the students in his group every week several hundred pages of the Harrison Textbook of Medicine to read and be prepared to answer questions in front of our peers the next Friday. That exercise turned out to be very useful, as I never thought I would have read all of that material if I had not been forced. Dr Grindon was fair, and he also demonstrated very high regard for each patient which he reinforced for all of us in his group. In effect, as he taught medicine, he also taught compassion and empathy. I looked back on that while I was on female ward service at the Brigham and realized I had learned something from Dr Grindon that I could now observe in Dr Hyslop. A highly intelligent and well trained as well as experienced physician can feel deeply human with regard to the patients in his or her care. Such physicians can feel true sorrow; they can laugh at times, and they can cry at times. Such a physician can recognize the risks involved in medical management but still proceed to do the right thing for the patient. The kind of activity that I observed as a junior student that really underscored these thoughts is epitomized by one night when I accompanied Dr Grindon to the bedside of an elderly man who was in an early stage of an acute myocardial infarction and had just developed rapid ventricular tachycardia. He told me what he was doing for this patient and quickly drew up a syringe of procainamide, a potent anti arrhythmic agent for IV use. As I looked from patient to my resident's face, I was struck by the beads of perspiration all over the doctor's forehead. That was when I focused on the fact that the resident knew there were huge risks involved for this patient and yet he did not hesitate to do what was needed at the time. It turned out the drug worked well and soon the patient returned to his normal cardiac rhythm. Only in retrospect and after a little more training myself did I realize that I now was working with a man with this same combination of compassion and competence in Newton Hyslop.

The patients admitted to E2F2 were nearly always over 30 years of age and many were quite elderly. They were family members or even the matriarch of a large family group. Taking care of these women meant very often discussing their progress with close family members. This was in 1966 and therefore long before all the regulations ostensibly designed to protest all aspects of patients' privacy. So, all I needed to do was clear with the patient my right to discuss aspects of their care that were appropriate for family to hear. There were times of course, when the patient would tell me not to disclose certain aspects of their history or care plans and I just like all my house officer colleagues always honored that request. As all physicians in training soon learn, it was inevitable that some sort of bond would form or even true friendship between me and some of these women. That was also somewhat true for family members who visited often and always had questions. I recall one very vivid example of all of this as an elderly Boston woman who I will call Mrs. C. was admitted to me with shortness of breath and fever. This lady had become ill with lots of coughing, fever, and yellow sputum. She was seen in the Emergency Room, had some lab work, was started on IV fluids and IV antibiotic, nasal oxygen and admitted to E2F2. The initial impression in the ER was that she had bilateral pneumonia and possibly also an element of heart failure although she had no prior history of heart disease. On arrival at E2F2, she seemed less anxious with the use of oxygen but still coughed a lot and brought up mildly thick golden yellow sputum. The initial lab studies revealed acceptable basic chemistries but a very high white blood count consistent with infection. Her exam showed no peripheral edema and no evident distension of her neck veins so there was no obvious evidence of any chronic fluid overload. The lungs were very noisy with very coarse breath noises and a few wheezes in the upper lung fields on both sides, and a crackling lower pitch raspy noise in her lower lungs. Her heart was regular and slightly rapid, but I could not hear any worrisome sounds like murmurs or gallop sounds as one might hear in cases of heart failure. The chest x-ray revealed a heart that was borderline large in overall size and patchy areas of whitish density in both mid and upper lung fields. We thought, as the ER team had suggested, that this was a woman with bilateral bronchopneumonia who probably also had some level of cardiac decompensation. She did appear to be somewhat improved from the previous notes on initial antibiotics, oxygen, nebulizer, and IV fluids. The antibiotic was selected in the ER empirically and I believe that was a penicillin plus very likely gentamycin to provide a good guess of broad coverage before there was any identification of the offending organism. The cultures obtained would take a little more time to complete. That was why Newton and I gathered a fresh sample of this lady's sputum and went to the small microbiology lab in order to see if we could get a better idea of the kind of bacteria involved. The usual practice then was to obtain a tiny bit of some possible fluid or mucous residue and streak it out on a microscopic slide in a very thin layer. That would then be fixed to the slide and then stained with coloring fluids to aid in microscopic identification. The commonest stain was the Gram stain which really helped as the bacteria and fungi that might cause infection were of two types, either Gram positive or Gram negative. This of course was based on whether the stain was taken up by the organism thus staining it or not. This would begin to put a given infecting agent into a category to help its identification. The gram stain together with a careful observation of the organisms under the microscope would give good clues to the identity of that "bug". So we prepared the slide and stained it and then soon had it under the microscope for a good look. Some micro-organisms tend to form in clusters, others in pairs, or singly. Some are odd shaped. Some have faintly visible clear coats that cover the organism like a glass shield. Newton and I were a little stunned because the organism under the microscope had features very suggestive of the Neisseria group. This is a group of pathogens that can cause infections and there are two large categories: Neisseria gonorrhoeae, one cause of sexually transmitted disease and then Neisseria meningitidis, a cause of serious forms of meningitis. We were at a loss to understand our findings as that did not fit at all what we were expecting, and we had no idea if Neisseria had ever really caused a bronchopneumonia. Since the patient did continue to improve, we elected to simply continue the current therapy including the antibiotics.

Early the next morning, there was a preliminary report from the bacteriology lab that suggested the organism was Neisseria meningitidis! We were faced with some real concern as this organism was very well known as a contagious and serious cause of meningitis. Did this lady have pneumonia and some heart failure due to this organism? Were her family at any risk of this infection spreading? Were any of the nurses or technicians or doctors who were in close proximity to this patient at some risk? As one would expect, there was a flurry of activity. I reexamined Mrs. C looking for any sign of a meningitis but found none and in fact she continued to look better. I think she did have a mild headache. We had discussions with this lady's family and no one else in the entire group was sick. No one had been sick. I myself had been home the night after admitting this lady so I called Johnny and learned that she and Anne were perfectly well. I told her to call me immediately if anything changed in that regard but really felt all was fine. I believe Newton and I decided to give a short course of penicillin to close family members of this patient as a prophylactic step.

Mrs. C continued to improve, and no other examples of this infection were uncovered. Newton and I started thinking about writing this case up for publication as it seemed so unusual and noteworthy. Sometime later, Newton did a lot of literature search I think on PubMed and discovered references in the literature to Branhemella catarrhalis and related organisms that can cause lower respiratory infection and can look like the organism Neisseria meningitidis. We abandoned our idea of publishing that article. Now, many years later it is clear that there was a lot of confusion about these groups of organisms and in fact we had one of the earlier cases in 1966.

Mrs. C continued to get better, and she turned into a really sweet, alert lady with warmth and a definite sense of humor.. I was really attached to this lady and also to her family. Some weeks after this admission and discharge, I received a package in the mail from this grateful family. In the package was a stone base that held a nice pen and mechanical pencil and on its base was engraved my name. If only these people knew, getting to know this lady and seeing her go from critically ill to well was way more reward for me than any gift.

During my time on E2F2 there was a very steady flow of new patients into the service with all kinds of complaints or ailments. Many were very complex and difficult to sort out but now and then there were some that appeared fairly easy to characterize. I recall one elderly woman admitted with a vague history of slipping and falling who had a series of bruises. On initial evaluation there was no clue to any kind of transient loss of consciousness. She did have several bruises and I didn't think they all looked like they were acquired at one time. That is, some of these had slightly different coloring as though they might be older than some of the others. Her husband visited and seemed quiet. He walked in using a cane for stability. I discussed this lady with several others including Dr Hyslop because of the unusual circumstances but also because some of the bruises had definite linearity-that is they had some length more than width. I could get no history of any kind of home problems from the patient. There also was no clue as to a cause of fainting or falling so the patient was discharged but I really didn't feel good about that outcome.

One night I was informed by the SAR that we were getting a transfer from the LCU as they were swamped with admissions. The patient in question was a very elderly and frail appearing lady who really did look ill. Based on her history, some of which I got and a lot of which came from the time in the LCU, she had suffered very recently an extensive anterior myocardial infarction. She had presented via the ER with chest pain but also evidence of some heart failure and mild confusion. On arrival at E2F2, she was on oxygen with high flow, and she had received a small dose of morphine as well as an IV diuretic with a central reliable IV line in place and also a Foley catheter. She had apparently responded to the IV diuretic as the Foley bag was full. This lady was feeble but seemed to understand directions and was cooperative with my exam. Her oxygen saturation was slightly low especially in view of the high flow oxygen via mask. Her blood pressure was marginal, but she did have palpable pulses in all four limbs. I could easily hear a systolic murmur that seemed to be mitral valve insufficiency. She had sinus tachycardia on the monitor, and she had a definite gallop sound on auscultation as seen in significant ventricular failure. I could listen to her lungs as she was propped up in bed and there were moist rales in both bases. We knew that this lady had already experienced several brief very fast rhythms thought to be bursts of ventricular tachycardia while she was in the LCU. These had apparently responded to IV lidocaine and she was on a continuous low dose drip of that medication in the hope of preventing that rhythm or worse. She was pain free and able to breath at rest with mild dyspnea sitting up with fast flow oxygen.

From the very start I think I realized this lady was really high risk, but I still was unclear about the fine line between getting by and suddenly crashing. I know I voiced my concerns to the SAR that night and I think Newton was off that night. I wondered why this lady had been transferred to us. It seemed the thinking was that this woman was very high risk and not a good candidate for any really heroic type of management. She might manage with cautious care if she survived for a day or so and there were many other patients with more favorable combinations of findings in whom advanced care really would likely help. This was the first time in my life that I really faced this lousy situation-at least the first time that it involved one of my patients.

I spent nearly the whole night in this lady's room. She was in the only single bedroom on E2F2 and very near the nursing station. She was continuously monitored with a bedside unit, and we had a defibrillator. We discussed the plan and opted for very tiny steps such as gradual changes on all therapies as she did seem like she was a little better than the way she was described on arrival in the LCU. Once while I was working with another patient in the ward, the nurse called me back to this lady's room because of an abrupt change of her rhythm on the monitor. I already mentioned the runs of ventricular tachycardia that had been seen in the LCU and the apparent good response from IV lidocaine. She was still on a low dose of continuous IV lidocaine but now had a very different rhythm that was wide and rapid. It was not at all clear if because of the low dose, the lidocaine was not adequate or alternatively, because of her age and decreased cardiac function and decreased liver blood flow where lidocaine was metabolized, the lidocaine had actually accumulated to a toxic range. I printed out a copy of her EKG rhythm and saw the rhythm was fast and wide, but it also was grossly irregular. At times there would be a slight decrease in rate and at those times the QRS from ventricular depolarization would be slightly narrower. I then knew she did not have ventricular tachycardia but had gone into rapid atrial fibrillation associated with some degree of left bundle branch block. That would explain the variation of QRS width as the rate slowed and the irregularity of the rate would be common with atrial fibrillation. Such a rhythm change would not be a surprise in the setting of a new large heart attack plus heart failure and mitral insufficiency. It also would probably not easily respond to electric shock with a cardioversion and it if did respond, it would very likely return to fibrillation since the severity of the heart damage and its failure were thought to be the causes of this rhythm. Therefore, we gave this lady a dose of IV digoxin, a digitalis drug that had as its early effects slowing of rapid conduction through the AV node from upper to lower chambers plus an increase in the vigor of heart muscle contraction. Within the next hour her heart rate did start to slow and with that the QRS became narrow once again. Before I could even rejoice at the apparent good effects of digoxin, the patient's condition then started to deteriorate right in front of me. Her blood pressure became lower and hard to hear with feeble pulses. The rest of that night is a huge blur as a lot was tried in a short time. I know blood was quickly sent to the lab to assess her chemistries, another small dose of diuretic was given, and she was placed on a low dose continuous IV levophed to raise the blood pressure. The blood potassium was in the lower end of normal range, but I gave a small IV dose of that substance anyway. We also intubated this lady so we could improve her lung function and possibly clear more fluid out of her lungs. There was progressive worsening with unresponsiveness, falling blood pressure, and finally a terminal ventricular fibrillation that would not respond to defibrillation or drugs. I know I worked longer than many would have but this was a very difficult situation for me. Finally, I was advised that further efforts were useless, and I should stop and then pronounce this little lady dead.

As I mentioned, my SAR Newton was off that night but the SAR who was there was of course very experienced, and he could see that I was upset. Some of what he said I don't remember, but he was fair and honest as he tried to give me some kind of support. There is really no easy way to handle such a problem. Lots of clinical experience does help a little and part of a human response is to try to soften the miserable feelings by finding reasons why all efforts would not have helped anyway. After some experience, I think many of us simply get able to quickly move on and think about other things. This is one of the hardest parts of being a physician. Later, when I had gotten home, my wife provided a soft sounding board. She said nothing but hugged me and just let me cry.

I feel like I should change the tone of this narrative a little so I will describe a little of the day-to-day activities on E2F2. As I probably mentioned before, one of the standards of care in those days was a very thorough history and physical exam. In the case of female patients and this was after all the female ward, there were times fairly often when a specific female pelvic examination was necessary. This was obviously true in any instance of suspected venereal disease to examine the pelvic area and vagina to look for evidence of infection and then to also obtain cultures of any area of concern to then later identify any organisms that would be pathologic and not just the normal vaginal flora. In other patients, the pelvic exam was at times somewhat less clear as to its real value, but it was part of a complete examination and would provide information about the lower abdomen and genito -urinary tract. In some cases, a normal pelvic examination merely served to help eliminate potential causes of a given complaint. Thus one can see there sometimes was a little thought as to whether this part of the exam was really needed at the time of admission. There were multiple examples where this decision to proceed with such an exam was often done just to be complete in the work up. For example, lower abdominal pain, vaginal discharge, painful menstrual periods, missed periods, and even conditions like a significant fever without a clear cause would lead to a pelvic examination. A little of the need to consider if this was necessary hinged on the time it took to set up and get it done, and especially how difficult it might be for the patient. The actual method of performing the pelvic exam in those days was a little archaic. The procedure and its need in a given case would first be explained to obtain patient consent. The patient with the help of the nurses would be positioned in bed on her back with sheets covering most of her body. Then a fresh bedpan which was shiny metal would be placed immediately under the patient's buttocks to support that part of her body and lift it slightly higher than the bed itself. This provided the examiner clear view of the pelvic structures and a clean field to allow insertion of the instrument used to open the vagina sufficiently to observe the cervix and if needed to swab the internal structures for samples of any fluid for microscopic exam and culture. A Papp smear would also be taken in this manner when it was appropriate. In my particular case, the methods of gently and carefully performing this entire exam had been covered using a fairly standard gynecologic exam table but the bedside method was shown to me by a senior resident with the aid of the nurses who always prepped the patient, tried to make her comfortable, assisted me with instruments, and remained with the patient the entire time of exam.

Because of the delay involved in setting it up, because it was time consuming, and possibly due to some feeling that the patient really was not totally at ease there were at times decisions made to hold off on this exam to see if it was really needed. This kind of delay could be a serious error if , as in a few instances in which time was important to solve a given problem. It also might result in some kind of critical comments from the SAR. As an aside, I am reminded of a small story involving the pelvic exam at the female ward that occurred about four years later, at the time when I was SAR on the E2F2. The service was very busy, and we all had put in long hours and had seen multiple problems. I felt that I needed a nap but going all the way back up the pike to my quarters was simply too far to be away that night. At about 4:30 AM I recalled seeing a typical gynecologic exam table being positioned up stairs on the corridor that connected part of Fmain to E2F2. I looked and found that bed and got onto it on my back and put my feet in the stirrups where I slept for nearly two hours. I was a little stiff but had managed a little sleep.

Somewhat similar was the approach to examination of the rectum and lower end of the colon, which was also done in the bed for males and females. A bedpan was used on those occasions where the exam had to be done with the patient supine. Many times, this lower colon exam could be done with the patient in a knee and chest position on their bed, so the bedpan was not needed. In those days the scope used to view the rectum and lower colon was a straight metal and silver colored tube about a foot long. It was somewhat uncomfortable for the patient, but it did provide a good view of parts of the lower GI tract otherwise not seen. I recall all the way back to my student years ,comments about the colonic or sigmoidoscopic exam with the designation "the silver telephone pole exam". Of course there now is a much better system for an even more complete exam of the colon using a flexible long colonoscope. This instrument can be carefully passed from the rectum all the way up to the start of the large bowel and has in its tip a tiny camera so the operator can view the colon all the way and thus see irregularities like polyps or cancers or ulcerations, etc. Even back in my early days, the silver telephone pole could provide very helpful information as the cause of rectal bleeding, lower abdominal pain, or abnormal stools. The evaluation of the entire colon back then might also require a barium enema in which the liquid barium mixture put into the colon from the rectum would allow the colon to be seen on x-ray. Similar studies are still available today with several refinements. So, this particular exam and its total value to patient care has also evolved over the years like all of medicine. I do recall a somewhat humorous but still quite embarrassing event a few years after my house officership. I was SAR on the female ward when my house officer called me to come as soon as possible to the bedside of his patient where he was trying to perform a rectal exam with a scope. I arrived to find the house officer and a nurse talking with a lady on her side with a sigmoidoscope seen protruding from her buttock region. The house officer explained that he had left the scope in place so I could see what he had found. So, with a few words to the patient, I leaned in and looked into that scope. In full view, I saw a normal appearing cervix! Even now, after all these years I give myself good marks for not chewing out the house officer or even laughing. I asked the house officer to lean in close with me and carefully study the area. Then I slowly withdrew that metal scope being careful to demonstrate from which orifice it was emerging. I had signaled to him to keep quiet, and he did. I then had the nurse assist me in getting this patient back into a seated position so I could speak with her. I explained that we had just done a brief exam of her genital tract and saw no evidence of any problem or cancer, but we still needed to get a good look at her lower bowel. Soon we were able to position her and try with a fresh sigmoidoscope to examine the rectum and lower colon finding no pathology. So she was again re assured that all looked fine and she was arranged in her bed as comfortable as possible. I took the house officer aside for a little discussion which he took fairly well although he was really embarrassed. In defense of this young man, the patient was definitely overweight and the exam in these circumstances was difficult. I also thought he had not had as much prior experience or training as he should have had. I believe there were many examples of all of us actually gaining needed experience as we did what seemed to be correct. I also submit that that is part of every internship or any other early phase of professional education.

As in previous sections of this memoir, I want to comment a little about the attending rounds and the group of physicians and scientists who gave them. The ward service for both male and female patients was directly under the management of the Medicine Department. So, technically, all such patients were the responsibility of George W. Thorn the Chairman of that department. The hierarchy from him down included Ting Kai Li as the chief resident in medicine, and then on each ward a senior assistant resident (SAR) who in turn had two house officers each to accomplish much of the evaluation and organization of care for these ward patients. As I have mentioned before, none of this could have happened were it not for a large group of well trained and very experienced nurses.

Formal day to day teaching was largely by way of early work rounds with the SAR to go over each patient and their problems plus their progress since arrival and then special time was spent with any new patients on the service. This would provide the SAR with information he would need to then present the new patients to Dr Thorn and others at Morning Report. At that particular session, all the new admissions from the night before were presented for discussion with Dr Thorn and usually several others including the

Chief Medical Resident. This did not only involve the patients on the ward service but all new patients in the hospital on the medical service. So, the JAR from the private service and the one from the Research Center would also briefly present their new patients. I am not sure whether JAR from the LCU presented those new patients or not as that unit was somewhat of its own entity and much of the day-to-day management was by way of the Fellows.

On an average day there would be so many new admissions that some would be presented at morning report only in brief. The bulk of the teaching for the house officers was done by the SAR going over their individual patients, plus regular attending rounds Monday, Wednesday, and Friday given by the ward attending physician for the month or fairly often by a guest attending for one day. As I recall, there were a few times when the attending duties were passed to a member of the faculty in one specialty or another to provide more variety and depth of the topics discussed. Thus during our time on the ward, Ralph and I had detailed sessions from physicians from other and adjacent parts of the Brigham system. This included representatives from the Boston Lying-In Hospital a few times, occasionally from the Robert Breck Brigham Hospital for Rheumatologic disease, infectious disease faculty people, and also faculty from cardiovascular medicine. At the time, there was a very active program at the Brigham and affiliated hospitals to study pulmonary embolism. There had been lots of animal and human research on this topic at the Brigham but also at the West Roxbury VA Hospital. This fit in well with presentations to us on many aspects of the management of thrombo-embolism. Dr James Dalin was a junior faculty member and one of Dr Dexter's fellows who gave us several lectures and or bedside sessions about pulmonary embolic disease. That brings me to an episode on the female ward service in my house officer year that directly involved Dr Lewis Dexter.

Dr Dexter was scheduled to be our attending on a given day and arrived together with several of his trainees and a student on elective with him. Knowing in advance that Dr Dexter who was widely respected for his work with cardiac catheterization including congenital heart disease as well as rheumatic heart disease, I selected one of my patients to present to him that I thought would be a good choice for discussion. This lady was a moderately obese woman in her late thirties who had been admitted with shortness of breath on exertion that had been progressive over the past year. She had no history of chest pain or lung disease but on questioning, she did describe a childhood illness said to be rheumatic fever. Her cardiac exam was difficult but in spite of distant heart tones, the first heart sound was fairly loud and sharp. I already knew then that a loud snapping first heart sound was commonly found in cases of rheumatic mitral stenosis so I thought this would be a good case for a very experienced clinician to review and discuss.

So, I presented this case to Dr Dexter and the group assembled with details of her history and I mentioned her heart tones were somewhat distant, but the first heart sound stood out as it was fairly loud and sharp. Trying to appear astute, I commented on the progressive dyspnea on exertion without elevated neck veins , peripheral edema, or rales in the lungs. Dr Dexter then took over by introducing himself to this lady and he tried to make her feel more at ease. He then went over with her some of her history and also spent a few moments talking about the illness she had in the past that was thought to be rheumatic fever. He then asked her if he could examine her heart and she agreed. He did do an exam and afterward stood up and spoke to all of us around the bed and to her. I have remembered that comment as it struck me as so unique coming from a well-known specialist in heart and valvular disease. He said something to the effect: "If this woman has heart disease, it could well be rheumatic mitral stenosis". Here was a remarkable and very experienced man being humble and truly honest with no excuses. The more I thought about that day, the more I appreciated Dr Dexter in that clinical context. I knew that it was not unusual for a diagnosis to be elusive so sometimes it might barely be suggested by one aspect of the history or exam. This underscores the absolute need to maintain a broad differential in formulating one's diagnosis.

There was a tradition at the Peter Bent Brigham Hospital and Harvard Med School nearly every year in the Spring. A renowned person from medicine or science from some other institution would be invited to come to Boston for about a week and serve as Physician In Chief, Pro Tem. This person would head up most of the teaching program and at the end of the week would give Grand

Rounds. This was a true highlight of the year for all at the Brigham. It was a marvelous opportunity to learn from someone who was far advanced in his or her career with very likely new or unusual aspects of their scientific thought. In February of 1966 Dr Thorn invited Dr Don Seldin from Texas University Southwest in Dallas as the PIC, Pro Tem. Dr Seldin was highly respected as an educator, administrator, and researcher. He was an excellent choice.

As per the usual custom for the PIC visit, Dr Seldin served as the visiting professor on each of the services for teaching rounds. I believe his schedule was planned so he could at least once visit each area of the hospital. He also heard the presentations all week at morning report with an overview of all the new admissions each day. On the Friday, he gave Medical Grand Rounds in the hospital amphitheater. All of these sessions were appreciated as they were in some ways fresh.

In addition to the formal part of the Physician In Chief visit, Dr Thorn used the occasion for some lighthearted fun and an excellent meal for the house staff and some faculty as I recall. The site for this dinner was the Tavern Club on Boyston in Boston. The Tavern Club had been in existence for years with facilities for large or small banquets but upstairs there was a complete theatre with stage, backstage, lighting, good acoustics, and seating for the audience. I believe membership in this club signified definite interest in excellent cuisine as well as live theatre. All sorts of presentations were given there over the years ranging from solo presentations to full and complete plays or operas. The Tavern Club was founded in 1884 and over those years was noted for its elite membership, such as Henry Cabot Lodge. Over the years a series of banquets with subsequent theatrical type presentations were given. Previous guests there included Mark Twain, Rudyard Kipling, John Singer Sargent, and Winston Churchill. For the PIC night, the tradition was an excellent dinner followed by a skit written and presented by the medical house staff. It was common to spoof the guest PIC person in a short play. As it turned out, there were several members of the Brigham house staff who were talented in music and singing as well as one or two with the wit and willingness to write lines for the play as well as the songs. As mentioned, this all focused on Don Seldin and as I remember, the lead in our play was played and sung by one of the SARs that I had not really met as yet-Shaun Ruddy. He got rave reviews, especially for belting out his song wearing a typical Texas ten-gallon hat!

I don't remember how any of us got off for that night, but I believe a cadre of older colleagues, fellows in local groups, and even a few faculty members took over our services for the night. The dinner was as expected, excellent. There was a very long banquet table with several courses and Dr Thorn had selected a superb wine: Chateauneuf du Pape. I was still at this time a wine novice but this one was really good- maybe a little too good as the glasses would be filled if they were emptied. Later I learned a little about that wine and that it took its name from the area near Avignon in the Rhone valley of France where Pope Clement V moved the papacy for a while. Apparently the soil and or general environment contributed to a highly scored red wine. I noticed that I was not the only one at dinner who then went upstairs feeling a little "loose". The show went very well, and it clearly was a program that I wish I had on tape to view it all again. It was funny and the music was really good. As I mentioned, Shaun Ruddy was fantastic as Don Seldin in a huge Texas style cowboy hat as he sang the songs.

Later, I was dropped off at my home and I was feeling no pain but still felt sorry that my wonderful wife had not been able to get out of the house and enjoy that evening and especially the meal. She was as expected, very curious about the evening and I did relate some of the highlights to her. We both knew, the meal would have been a wonderful experience for us as a couple, but the show was so closely linked to medicine and to the Physician In Chief that a lot of that would have been lost on her.

I have in previous sections described the constant battle with inadequate sleep but before I leave this section on E2F2 I want to add a story that my colleague, Bill Grossman provided for this book. Bill was on his rotation on E2F2 one night and after being on duty about forty busy hours, he got a new admission in the form of an elderly lady who was being evaluated for some kind of shortness of breath and vague chest pains. Bill dutifully obtained a very detailed history and then explained that he wanted to do his physical examination. This lady had been in the hospital before and was quite familiar with the procedures, so she readily agreed. Bill told me he was exhausted but he proceeded almost by habit. At the point of mid exam, while listening with his stethoscope over this woman's chest ,bill actually fell asleep!. This lady was immediately aware of what had happened but still amazingly relaxed. She looked at Bill and told him to go get some sleep since she would still be there in the morning. I understand that Bill recalled this episode and then related it to me at least in part out of embarrassment. I think this episode is a nice way to finish this chapter on female ward medicine as it basically speaks for all the house officers of our era.

The next rotation for me was the emergency room and that was now fast approaching. That would be quite different than nearly living for weeks on E2F2. It would also put me in the position of seeing the acute illnesses first and with the SAR initiating the management. I went to each of my patients on E2F2 and explained that I was rotating off that part of the hospital and a new team of doctors would take over in the morning. There were as usual a few patients who appeared worried about this abrupt change, but I told them the new people coming onto the service were well versed in their individual problems and were very good. I assured these patients they would see how really good these house officers and residents   were   for   themselves.

CHAPTER FIVE: Emergency Room

When I arrived at the Emergency Room early on my first day it was perfectly clear that this would be a very different experience from in hospital management. I of course already knew from past experience as a med student that there would be a daily exposure to multiple people with a wide variety of complaints or problems. Some of these people would have been sent there from a private physician, others from other institutions in the general Boston area, and many new patients would have not had very much or any previous medical attention. In effect the whole gamut of well off and previously well nurtured patients to those with little or no previous medical care was covered. Some patients would be seen in the ER with pure surgical problems or with pure medical type ailments and there would be many with mixed needs or at least unclear initial presentation. As new patients arrived at the ER, they were all triaged by a senior nurse into medical or surgical service and directed to the appropriate area of the ER for initial evaluation and care. Overlap situations could often be easily managed by a quick consult from a member of the other group be it medical or surgical. As I look back on that time, I realize that within the general area of the Brigham were several specialty hospitals and they had some emergency facilities. Thus, in general all obstetrical or gynecological acute problems were taken to the Boston Lying In hospital. To a certain extent, some types of urgent care were routed away from the Brigham ER like for example acute eye injuries went directly to the Massachusetts Eye and Ear Hospital, and some acute psychiatric problems would go directly to the Massachusetts Mental Health Hospital.

As soon as I arrived to start my first day, one of the nurses took me on a tour of the entire Emergency Room. This included the actual nursing station, the surgical area, the medical area, and rooms for special problems such as major trauma, cardiac arrest, or need for isolation because of potential infectious diseases. This was my introduction not only to the physical facilities of the ER but also the nursing support. As a first-year resident, I quickly learned to really appreciate the assistance of the ER nurses who in general had a lot of previous experience with the myriad of different types of disease. Of course, as the house officer I also had direct support and back up from my assigned SAR.

The entire Brigham Emergency Room was in the midst of major renovation at the time and so a few areas were blocked off by signs or tape and I believe there were some areas still being finished from all the redecoration. Thus, it happened, that some patients due to the pressing need for evaluation and care were seen in areas that were not finished in the renovation. There was an episode that I vividly recall very early in my ER rotation when a very agitated and confused woman grabbed a loose piece of wood off the wall where it was partially attached . This wooden runner was specifically there to protect the walls from being hit by equipment or gurneys, However, since it was not completely fixed to the wall this lady was able to pull it off and then wield it like a weapon. She screamed and waved that piece of wood around to threaten anyone who might get close to her. All of us noticed the commotion and a few of the nurses with a surgical house officer had a brief discussion ,I assume about how to handle the problem. Then abruptly, the surgical house officer stepped forward towards the patient and in a firm voice said: "You can't do this, give that to me!" The patient obliged by whacking him on the side of the head whereupon, two nurses grabbed the patients' arms and took some level of control. There was a scuffle, but the nurses won and very soon another arrived with a needle and syringe and administered to the patient an intramuscular injection of some kind of sedation. After a few minutes the patient was quiet and seemingly asleep. They checked her vital signs and then moved her to another cubicle for more thorough evaluation. The surgical house officer did require a few stitches to close a laceration on the side of his head but otherwise was OK. I thought he probably learned a good lesson about confronting someone with a weapon. As I look back on this episode, I think it was a lot like a snippet from a Laurel and Hardy movie!

The level of activity in the Emergency Room was nearly constant and at times very serious. Meals were often in the form of snacks on the run. I did learn later that Bill Grossman's wife, Melanie sometimes brought him a meal from home while he was on his rotation to the ER. They lived fairly close to the hospital.

The shear variety of problems was at once both stimulating and challenging. Some of these were also quite depressing. There were patients brought in by ambulance with little evidence of life and sometimes there were vigorous attempts at resuscitation both with and without success. There was one time when a young woman was brought in comatose due to a self-ingested bottle of pills. She was resuscitated and stomach gavaged but within an hour there was a second similar admission of another woman somewhat older. That second patient also had taken a bottle of her pills in a suicide effort, and she was in fact the mother of the first patient! These two women did have previous visits to the Brigham and had extensive records which included previous deliberate overdoses. There was a prompt response from the psychiatric person on call and it turned out he knew both of these patients. I believe both of these ladies survived this crisis.

On one of my very early days in the Brigham ER, the place was very busy with all the cubicles filled and a group of at least 10-12 people seated on a long bench waiting to be seen. As I hurried from one cubicle to another, I felt someone grab my coat to stop me. I looked at this man and he immediately started frantically telling me I had to help him right away. He told me he was feeling like he would have a fit. He admitted he was a barb addict but insisted he had been trying to kick the habit except now he felt he was going to have another fit like he had experienced in the past. I explained to this fellow that I couldn't help him until I got him checked into the ER and received his records, but he should sit down and try to be calm, and he would be attended very soon. Out of my level of inexperience, I was a little worried about this man, but I also felt totally swamped and decided I had to get back in sequence with all the people awaiting care. I went to the next cubicle to see my next new patient but within only a very few minutes, I heard one of the nurses yelling at me to come back to the waiting area where there was a patient with a seizure! I quickly turned to go back to the front of the ER and thought "Oh my God! That man told me he needed help right away and I left him." Sure enough it was the same man who had tried to get help from me, but he was now on the floor with a series of jerking motions of his limbs and some spittle running out of his mouth. His eyes were open, but they did not seem to focus on anything and he did not respond to me or the nurses. I asked one of the nurses to draw up for me a dose of phenobarbital for IM use in a syringe as I tried hard to get a padded tongue blade into this man's mouth to protect his airway .tongue, and his teeth from seizure activity. It was at this point that I became aware of a tall man who had come right up to this man on the floor and stood right next to him. As I looked up and was going to stop this apparent by-stander, the tall man reached out with the point of his shoe and poked my patient in the side of the ribs and said in a loud voice "Get up! Come ON, Get Up!" I think I was shocked and a little horrified, but I then realized the tall man was one of the Brigham Senior Residents, Dr Nelson Trujillo! I then heard him say in a loud voice :"We need a spinal tap here, so set it up and bring me the large needle!" Miraculously, the patient stopped jerking, started moving and sat up. In the previous moments, I had managed to get a blood pressure on this man and so I could quickly see that he had normal pressure and a regular heart rate. The patient was helped up and then seated on the nearby bench as the crowd started breaking up. Dr Trujillo took over and talked with the patient. He was assisted by two of the ER nurses while another nurse signaled me to step aside. She then told me the man I had encountered was truly a barbiturate addict but also had been in the ER before in an effort to receive a dose of drug. She took me to the nurses' station there in the ER and pulled out a large hard bound book that had a label on the front: Kook Book. Inside were all kinds of brief accounts of unusual situations seen in the ER before ,concerning malingers, drug seekers, and other so called "frequent fliers", who had some kind of ulterior motive for their visit to the emergency room. With minimal searching, the nurse found for me a page describing my patient. His method was to present to the ER early in the month so he could encounter a somewhat green house officer who had not seen him before. In general, this man was fairly convincing as he had twice managed to get some kind of barbiturate injection before being identified. Later, Nelson Trujillo stopped by and took me aside briefly. He told me he was simply cutting through the emergency room when he recognized the patient as a problem patient and decided to step into the management. He told me, I would for sure encounter other patients who would fake some kind of illness to achieve something whether it might be hospital admission, lots of attention, or as in my case some kind of medication. Over a few years, that was correct and I did encounter several individuals who claimed illness or even acted out a little scene to get something. That would include a few people who feigned illness with fever even to the point of finding a way to suddenly acquire a rise in their body temperature. After a while, I like other physicians picked up a slight sense of doubt in some cases based on previous experiences. I will say this though: If you are a caring person, you will pay a price yourself every time you deal with a patient who wants and claims to need some kind of care but you have reasons to doubt that and therefore choose what appears to be the right course based on the available evidence.

A lot of what happened in the emergency room depended heavily on the triage system that I mentioned above. At any given time, there nearly always were at least a few people sitting on the bench waiting to be seen and fully evaluated. The nurses saw all patients on arrival with the intent of placing each of them in a sequence of patients to be seen based on their apparent or potential severity. Because there was a constant influx of new patients, this group who sat and waited was constantly changing. On a few occasions, a given person would need to be reevaluated by the triage team if for example, they seemed more seriously ill. Some patients arrived by ambulance and in general these were seen promptly and placed often in a cubicle for evaluation. Some patients were obviously seriously threatened, and they would also go immediately to a cubicle or specialized room for urgent management. This latter group included major trauma, comatose individuals, patients in shock, patients post cardiac arrest or acute myocardial infarct as well as others with critical problems. As I mentioned earlier, the triage nurses would also direct each new patient to a medical or surgical team. In the case of overlap of a patient's problems with medical and surgical implications, they would be started on one service but with consult type help from the other service.. It was quite common for me to ask one of the surgical residents to see a patient for me briefly to acquire their opinion for example concerning abdominal pain or some kind of injury. I in turn was often asked to listen to a patient's heart sounds or interpret an EKG for one of the surgical residents.. This kind of working together was important and very helpful for me as well as the patients. I did have the impression that there was a little too much competitiveness at times and there is no place for any kind of turf wars in an emergency setting. I also got input from the SAR in the emergency room. I recall one patient for whom this medical and surgical interplay was important. This was a middle-aged man brought to the ER after falling off a ladder. It was not clear whether he lost his balance, or tripped, or possibly briefly passed out. He was directed to me because there was no major obvious trauma and he had some kind of fall or passing out with a background history of hypertension, diabetes, and mild renal impairment. This man was fully awake but didn't remember the actual fall. He denied any prior falls or fainting spells and also did not recall any kind of light headedness or dizziness prior to falling. There was no history of chest pain or other warning signals prior to going up on the roof. There also had been no signs of blood loss or fever. He thought his blood sugar should be fine as he was on a diet and an oral agent for control and had not had any problems with his sugar level in the past. His blood pressure was slightly elevated when I first saw him but within a short time of continued questioning and some reassurance from me, a repeat pressure was lower, so it did not need specific medication at the time. The stat blood sugar was in normal limits after a finger stick had indicated the same thing. His lab studies also did not reveal any significant abnormality of the basic chemistries including his renal function. He did have several abrasions and one ankle was tender and in addition he was quite tender over the left lower rib cage anteriorly. I ordered x ray studies of the ankle and also chest with close views of the anterior ribs. I saw several other patients while this man was in radiology department and when he returned there was a preliminary report that indicated no fractures. For some reason that I don't recall, I repeated his physical exam and it seemed that he was even more tender in the left upper quadrant of the abdomen. I knew there were no fractures, and the patient did have good bowel sounds and normal pulses in both legs. So, I asked for a surgical consult and ordered more x-rays-specifically a flat plate of the abdomen and then an upright film also of the abdomen. That is a very common type study to evaluate abdominal complaints as it shows the position of the gas filled bowels, some major organs, and if there is some kind of bowel perforation with gas leaking out of bowels and into the abdominal cavity it shows up as thin line of free air that otherwise is never normal. The surgical resident did a quick exam and agreed on the need of those x-rays. The patient was quickly taken to radiology for these films and returned to the ER. When I next saw this man he looked anxious and was sweaty. His blood pressure had dropped to 100/70 as I recall. His abdomen was clearly more tender, so it was clear there was a very significant problem. I thought this man had a ruptured spleen based on the history of a fall, the location of his tenderness, and then a definite fall of blood pressure. At this point, the patient became much more seriously ill as the heart rate went up and blood pressure fell. He was placed in a shock position and IV fluids opened up for rapid flow. As soon as possible we received some blood for transfusion from the blood bank and as soon as his blood pressure came up a little, he was taken directly to the operating room. He did have a lot of free blood within the abdominal cavity and a ruptured spleen. Bleeding was controlled, blood was given, and the spleen was removed. He then was on the surgical service and taken to the ICU in the Bartlett unit. This man survived without further complications. I checked on him the next day and he seemed to be doing well. As always in a situation like this one, I mulled it over in my thoughts for several times. I couldn't imagine why I had repeated his exam after his first trip to the radiology unit with no evidence of fractures. I came to believe, that there was some subtle indication that this man was sicker, but I could not specifically describe it. I did believe and to some extent I still believe there are at times such very subtle signals of potential disaster one might pick up by being very alert. I know I have learned of other physicians who have had very similar experiences.

Mixed in with the myriads of patients were several good examples of illness or injury related to drugs and or alcohol. Such problems were every bit as common in 1966 as they are today but there are several "new players" such as fentanyl. As a student I had seen several examples of patients who were intoxicated, nauseated, or injured in some way due to excessive alcohol intake. The emergency room experience at the Brigham provided many more examples of alcohol related illness but also a strange mix of various chemical agents sometimes with alcohol and sometimes as the sole cause of a patient's altered mental state with or without physical evidence of disease or dysfunction. There are always patients in this general category and some of them can be very uncooperative and actually belligerent. Such patients represent a special problem for each medical or surgical practitioner simply because of the difficulty of sorting out ailments mixed in with total lack of cooperation. This is especially the case when there is by history or exam some reason to consider some serious illness presenting under the guise of alcohol excess. It is clear that to evaluate such a patient fully will require some kind of sedation which in itself carries some risks. For example, I recall a man admitted via the emergency room to me for evaluation of confusion and minor injuries associated with a fight in a local bar. This man had several abrasions and a small amount of blood coming from a tiny cut on his lower lip. However, he was very unreasonable and demanding to the point that I felt threatened and stood back slightly as I tried to introduce myself and start to get some history. He got very loud and basically dared me to come closer. I think one of the nurses actually suggested the use of some type of calming medication and I agreed. So, this fellow received an IM injection of a small dose of Haldol as I recall. It only took a few minutes for him to relax and quit yelling and soon he was totally relaxed to allow a careful exam. He did not seem to have any serious injuries; his vital signs were acceptable including temperature and finger sensor oxygen content of blood. I could not find any local area of swelling or tenderness on his limbs and the chest and abdomen seemed also benign. So he would not need a major work up but would need admission to the hospital to allow him to detoxify what we now knew was a high blood alcohol level. He was accepted on the psychiatry service since they knew him from previous admissions. I admit I was relieved to transfer his care.

It is really difficult to accurately depict the hectic pace of working in that ER. While there was here and there a quiet time, they were few in number and surrounded with multi-patient chaos. On nights off I would get home exhausted and hard to describe but mentally as well as physically tired. I think Johnny believed she was married to a zombie. She always listened to my tales of ups and downs from the day before and I seemed to be a little more relaxed by telling her what I had seen and done. As I mentioned earlier, I still tried to leave out some episodes in order to spare her a little because some were grisly or very depressing in their final end point.

Thus, a lot of the activities involving serious bleeding, failed resuscitation, pain, and death were not shared in my home counseling unit.

There were in truth, a few patients that I saw in the Brigham ER and now can look back with a grain of humor even though at the time, there was nothing funny about their plights. One of these was a very likeable 45-year-old man who presented to the desk at the entrance to ER complaining of pain in his knee. The time was 4:30 AM. I was at the tail end of a two-day shift that had been very stressful, and I was very tired. The ER had gotten fairly quiet and so I could actually lay down in an empty cubicle and get a nap. The nurses were supporting of this idea when it happened, and they were really good at letting me know if there was a new patient. So, on this particular night, I was awakened by one of the nurses who said there was a new patient all signed in and waiting to see me. Now I would like all who read this memoir to try to imagine the scene. When I got to the right cubicle, I met a fairly nice fellow who did not seem to be in any distress. He was dressed in workman type clothes and was seated with one leg of his pants rolled up to reveal his left knee. The knee was definitely swollen and possibly slightly pink in the color of the skin. His vital signs were all normal. In the course of obtaining the history I learned that the knee had been painful for about two months, sometimes more than others. It had been swollen and at times slightly red in appearance. There was no history of any kind of injury or trauma. I asked him if the knee was progressively getting worse and he said that it was really about the same. At that point, I looked him in the eye and asked why he had come in tonight for care of the knee. He told me he was driving down Huntington Avenue and he saw our sign lit up for the emergency room, so he decided to drive in and have the knee checked. I think I was a little chagrined or stunned but I did not vent any feelings on this man as he was so nice and quite human, and after all it was very clear that he had a real problem with that knee. I did give him a brief comment about never putting off getting medical attention for such an ailment and mentioned that many conditions are easy to manage if caught early but can be huge problems if not seen until complications set in. This patient was seen by a surgical resident who helped me with a joint aspiration since there clearly was excess fluid in the joint space. The fluid was yellow and cloudy but there was no bleeding. Samples of fluid were sent to the lab for culture and smear on microscopic slide as well as several chemistry analyses. The patient had a septic knee, but I didn't have a clue where it had come from. The obvious things for me were all negative such as trauma, known skin infections, bites, venereal disease, etc. The man actually did well in the hospital on antibiotics and I checked on him two days later. I realized that many people for whatever reason, put off seeking medical help in spite of all kinds of new problems. I also came to realize this was much more common in males than females and in fact over the years I recognized many times that a man was seeing me largely at the insistence of his wife or girlfriend.

The rotation in the emergency room passed quickly. It was about this time that I had to report to the US Army and begin my military service. Thus, I started to go to the base for weekend training every other weekend. That markedly decreased my time to be actually off duty and cut into time at home on those weekends that should have been off. The hours at the base were Saturday and Sunday from about 8 AM to 5 PM so I still had a little time in the evenings to be with my family. I chose to put this chapter of my memoir in at this juncture because the Army duty did begin for me and my time away from home did change at this point. I finished up my rotation in the ER, said good by, and left the staff two bags of donuts. Then I was off to my last rotation of the house officer year on the Male Ward, F Main. But first, let me insert this part of the story that deals with the U   S   Army   Reserves.

CHAPTER SIX: The U.S. Army Reserves

Experience as a member of the armed services was never even imagined by me as I went through medical school although there were a few people in my class that had such experience or who would face it in their future. How it came to pass that I would become an officer in the Army Reserves in the Medical Corps was actually fairly simple. The war in Viet Nam was hot and heavy with daily accounts in the newspapers and it seemed it would not stop soon. It also seemed likely that physicians would be needed. As I got a few months into my first year at the Brigham, there were already a few of my schoolmates over there in combat areas. In addition, there was a story I had heard at St Louis U. Med School of a physician who was drafted in some way for active duty even though he had moderately severe asthma. I don't know who that was or even if it is a true story, but it is the type of gossip we all heard at that time.

During my first months at the Brigham, I had more than enough to keep my mind busy without considering whether I could be called up for some reason and thus interrupt my training. When these ideas did come up, I really thought I was safe since I was in a very good training program at a well-regarded institution, and I had a wife and a small baby. At the time, there was a very strong tradition at the Brigham that after you completed your junior resident (JAR) year of training, you would go away for some kind of advanced training. That could be in a research setting or clinical experience but after completing that activity you would return to the Brigham as a Senior Resident (SAR). This was one of the real strengths of the Brigham because the SAR would have at least two years of further training and experience more than the JAR and thus would be a full three years more experienced than the house officers. Many of these advanced training positions would result in the in-depth experience needed to become board certified in a medical subspecialty. Many of the physicians who finished their JAR year went on to accept a position at the National Institutes of Health or the Communicable Disease Center. I think this entire system of leaving for a while and then returning to the Brigham actually was started many years before and possibly by Dr Henry Christian himself. Dr Henry A. Christian was the first Physician in Chief at the Brigham Hospital. I should point out that being accepted to NIH or CDC for further training carried with it an appointment to the Public Health Service and therefore was an actual commission thus taking the recipient out of the possibility of draft. I think in general those commissions as well as appointments of individuals into formal Fellowship training in a subspecialty resulted in draft deferment whereas a general residency might not.

As I recall, I was told to report to the Director of the Medical Residency at the Brigham, Dr Eugene Eppinger. I believe that happened in the early Fall of 1965. I already knew a little about Dr Eppinger and that he was a true gentleman very well-liked by the house staff as well as the faculty. Everyone at the Brigham affectionately referred to him as "The Epp". When I arrived at his office, it was immediately clear that he wanted to talk about my future career in medicine. He asked what my plans were for a career and specifically what I planned for the time after my JAR year. I confessed that up to that time I had spent very little time actually considering those issues. Dr Eppinger then went on to point out that not only was some kind of advanced training the norm after the JAR year but that there also currently was a real risk that I could be called up for military duty since the war in Viet Nam was boiling over and there would no doubt be more physicians needed. He then brought up the possibility of an appointment at the National Institutes of Health or the Communicative Disease Center both of which were very popular among Brigham residents and also very good training. Each of those positions carried with it a full commission in the US Public Service and thus eliminated the recipient from any kind of draft. I told him I was aware of those positions, but so far I was still uncertain about what subspecialty of medicine I wanted to pursue. He told me to think about it some more and possibly do some searching for more information but then to return to see him in two weeks for more discussion.

I soon discussed this meeting and its implications with Johnny who was not only my life partner but also my really valuable sounding board. She was well aware of my feelings about signing up for the cardiology fellowship with Dr Bernard Lown. She and I had hashed that out multiple times. I did feel a strong pull toward cardiology and in fact also to Dr Lown and his methods of patient care. I was not swayed by his fellows who seemed to be telling me how difficult the fellowship could be and how tough Dr Lown was as a boss. I decided to go back to the Lown office for more interviews and was as before, given a fairly solid impression that my application would be well received. Johnny and I talked about little else in the time before my next meeting with Dr Eppinger. We both had called parents but neither set really pushed us except to indicate they wanted what was best for us and yes, they would prefer I was not in a war zone. I realized that my mom and dad were on my side, but they really could not really weigh all the factors involved in this decision, so I did not expect them to take a definite stand. Johnny's parents also made no strong stand on this choice but if any moving was involved they wanted it to be back to St Louis.

I reported back to Dr Eppinger and the discussion was re started. However, this time I told him I was really thinking about remaining in Boston and signing up for the Cardiology Fellowship with Dr Bernard Lown. I further explained that I had discussed this a lot with my wife who was very supportive. I told him we had a baby, and we really liked our home and the neighborhood. We didn't relish moving and starting all over again. Dr Eppinger then told me about something that he had just learned and that was the US Army was forming a reserve unit in Boston and was looking for physicians. If I joined the Army Reserve, I would be free of getting drafted. There would still be a chance that the unit could be called for active duty but that did not seem likely. I told him that I would look into the possibility of joining that unit. It looked like I would remain in the Brigham for my next phase of training.

There was once again a lot of concern and discussion between Johnny and I about our immediate future. In the end, we made the decision to sign up for the Lown Fellowship and to talk with the Army recruiter about that unit. And so, Richard Whiting who had never even considered a military career signed up and became Captain Richard Whiting in the 373rd General Hospital, US Army Reserve, Boston, Massachusetts. What I didn't know at that time was this unit was planned to be a fully functional general hospital. If there was a specific need, the unit could be activated and sent anywhere to fill that need. Further, this unit was designated as a Special Reserve Force or SRF. That meant that the 373rd General

Hospital was to be always ready to pack up and go wherever needed and that in turn meant we would have twice as many meetings as the regular reserve units. For the Whiting family, that translated into me being at the military base in Boston every other weekend on Saturday from 8 AM to 5 Pm and again on Sunday the same hours. Readers will recall that at the time my duty call at the Brigham was every other day and every other weekend. So it dawned on Johnny and I that we would have much less time together at home once the Army training started. That would be still a few months away.

There were a few benefits from being in the reserves and attending the training sessions. The biggest of these was of course that I was paid as a Captain and that turned out to be a huge benefit especially with twice a month Army duty. We got to the point where we no longer had to borrow money from The Franklin Foundation or any other group. There also was a sort of a benefit for officers like me since we were all from medical or surgical training programs centered in Boston. With that many residents or fellows in training, we were able to set up a series of lectures for ourselves over and above the lectures required by the Army. We all took turns giving presentations and that way regularly heard about other specialties and in effect a lot of fairly new therapies. There were plenty of classes, practice drilling, learning military procedures, etc. Each summer, the unit would be put on active duty for two weeks of training at an Army base. For our unit, that was often at Camp Drum in upper New York State, or Fort Dix in New Jersey. The former was fairly crude with old barracks and hospital buildings literally in the middle of deep woods. As a functional hospital unit, we would take over and run the hospital including the Emergency room, medical and surgical units, pharmacy, laboratories, and any other hospital type needs. When we went to a major facility like Fort Dix, we would be inserted into an active hospital to work side by side with the full-time personnel and even sometimes worked in dependent outpatient clinics. I don't intend to belabor that formal experience, but it did provide a very good introduction to base medicine and surgery. I will tell one short story from my time at Fort Dix when I was assigned to the Dependent Outpatient Clinic. This episode is firmly in my memory. Let me start by saying, my experience was really quite good on these assignments, and I do not intend to make anyone think the care and management were anything but quite effective. However, there was one episode that as I said is locked in my memory. The man who was permanently assigned to that clinic was clearly overloaded with patients. The system was based on anyone who was on the base as a dependent of an active-duty serviceman could decide to see the doctor and simply go to the clinic before hours and sign up. So, when the clinic opened in the morning there would be a long list of patients to be seen that day and many would already be there in waiting. This system to me now years later was really much like the one that has evolved in many offices today. The physician is in a situation in which there are too many patients and too many patient complaints or illnesses to manage in a short time. So, that means, the physician has to manage somehow. Sometimes he or she would have a reservist show up for two weeks and it was obvious to me they loved seeing help arrive. Most of the time, the physician would hurry through an evaluation and try to do the best they could. That entire system of hurry up medicine is always destined to result in mistakes or less than ideal care in my opinion. That gets me to the case I have in my memory. I had reported for duty at this clinic and was amazed at the shear numbers of patients to be seen. There was a young woman brought in by her mother because of listlessness and weakness. She just did not feel well on any day. When I looked at this young woman, she was very pale and that included her mucous membranes in the mouth as well as the lines in her hands. It was obvious to me that this girl was anemic. She had been seen in that clinic I think on two previous occasions for weakness and fatigue. The records were sparse, but it seemed that the focus of previous visits was on whether this girl was depressed. I couldn't find any lab data in the chart. I asked about her menstrual periods and learned that they were very heavy and seemed even more so in the last two months. From that point I was certain this woman was seriously anemic from excessive menstrual bleeding. She was not on any medications. As the readers of this will guess, this young woman had a hemoglobin in the range of 8 and a very low serum iron level. When I told the physician in charge of the clinic about this case, he was clearly sad, and I think felt bad but didn't try to make any excuses. It was obvious to me that the rapid-fire system of care led to a lot of hurry up thoughts and could easily have been mistakenly managed. I never got any long term follow up on this young woman, but I do know she was put on Iron therapy and referred to the OB Gyn clinic.

On weekends at the base, we often had classes and sometimes were taken outdoors for practice with marching and all the maneuvers related to that. There was at least one time when we were loaded into a series of buses and taken to a firing range. We had lectures primarily concerning weapon safety but also a little about the common weapons themselves. As officers, we were trained primarily with the .45 caliber Colt pistol. Finally we were taken to the actual firing range where there were a series of small wooden stands lined up where each of us stood more or less side by side. We were issued the pistols and I was amazed at the weight of that gun. The instructors went up and down the line and made us handle the weapon and demonstrate how to insert the ammunition clip. We were given a clip of live ammunition and told to load the weapons and then slide the barrel back once to actually load the first round into the firing chamber. We were instructed how to stand firm and hold the weapon lined up on the target. The gunnery sergeant then told us to commence firing and continue until our ammo was depleted and then to put the gun on the stand. He may have had us all fire one or two rounds to get the feel of the gun firing and I was totally amazed at that feeling of power. Anyway the firing was loud and was completed soon but I then saw to my right, one of the nurses had her weapon jam after a few shots. She brought the gun back toward her body to look at it and started to ask for help. However, as she brought the gun closer it was pointed directly down the line of shooters including me. The drill sergeant screamed and hurried to her side and basically pulled the gun out of her hand and pointed it down to the ground. There then was a long and somewhat heated talk about the safety we were supposed to understand and what to do if a gun jammed. He included the awareness of where one's weapon was pointed at all times. Well, that nurse was mortified. She was however a reservist for several years and had actually had full training in the past. That episode on the firing range did impress me and I think most of the rest of us on the line that day. I don't recall any other actual firing type training, but I did enjoy the shooting itself and years later would go to a range and fire at targets.

The first summer camp in the Army for me was the summer of 1966 which was immediately after I finished my house officer year. I received orders to report to the Naval base in Boston harbor where we had all of our weekend meetings. We all gathered dressed in fatigues and with duffel bags or in some cases small suitcases with extra clothes and toiletries. Soon we were put into a large formation and stood at ease for a while. There were several buses lined up and we were directed to get on board. Soon the buses pulled out of the base headed for the long ride through Massachusetts and into New York State. After a long ride the buses left the highway which really reminded me of riding in Missouri because of the heavy tree cover and variable hills. The buses in line went onto a much smaller road and continued for some time. Then we approached the gate leading into Camp Drum with several guards, a fence, and the kind of gate that blocked the road but could be raised to let vehicles pass.

While we sat there waiting to be cleared to enter the base, I noticed a wooden building off to the left side. It looked like an old ranch house, and I would estimate it was approximately 200 yards away from the actual army base. I learned later that this was a sort of a strip club set up outside the base to entertain the troops. I would guess that every military base has something like that to provide drinks and some form of entertainment. More on this place will be covered a little later in this memoir.

After a while, the buses were cleared to proceed into the camp and back into a heavily wooded area. That soon gave way to more developed areas with some buildings and eventually the buses pulled into a large open area in front of the Camp Drum Base Hospital. All the hospital facilities were in this area and nearby were several old barracks in which both the officers and the enlisted men would be bunked. These were separate buildings but otherwise similar. The officers had somewhat better quarters in that we each had a single bed in a small room with a small table and chair. There was an adjoining small building that was for bathroom and shower facilities that were shared. For the enlisted men, I believe they were bunked side by side and double bunked in a large room which also had its own bathroom and clean up facilities.

These buildings were old and that showed. They were made of wood and the white paint was heavily peeling off all the walls. They were built up one or two feet above the ground so there was a small empty space under each that had a lot of weeds. We were spread out off the buses and then taken to our assigned barracks to be settled. The bed was a single, but it was clean and quite acceptable.

The next morning quite early there was bugle playing-I think by a loud recording-to get all of us started on our first day of active duty in the Army Reserve. This was clearly a very different experience for almost all of the officers at least than any of our past. This first morning was in fact pretty much the same as all the others, always starting with reveille. All of us would get up and head for the bathroom area to shower, shave, and get ready for duty. Then it was off to the mess hall for breakfast. The food was fine and there was plenty for the large group. Then we would go to our individual duty stations and as I recall my first assignment was on the medical ward in charge of hospitalized patients. Each ward had a desk at it entrance which actually was the nursing station. There were two rows of beds each running the length of the room to a second doorway at the far end. The beds were parallel with each other and separated by about 2-3 feet with the head end on the windowed wall and the foot end facing inward across from the bed on the other side of the room. Each bed had a small receptacle on the foot end to hold a folding metal chart with the records for that particular patient. The nurses could fill in vital sign charts and the doctors could write admission notes, progress notes, etc.

As we all expected, the actual number of hospitalized patients was always fairly light even though the criteria for admission were deliberately set fairly low so there would be patients for the hospital to serve and to give experience to many of the enlisted men. There might be patients admitted with gastro-intestinal complaints, fevers, minor infections, or injuries. As I mentioned earlier, we were designated as a full-service hospital and so when someone was admitted with for example, an orthopedic problem, they would be seen by an orthopedic surgeon as a consult. There were always a few men admitted with headaches, but they usually were in and out of the hospital fairly rapidly. Now and then, we would receive a more significant injury. One that was new to me was a young enlisted man who jumped down from a heavy vehicle but caught his ring on some part of the vehicle as he dropped down to the ground. That resulted in the ring acting like a shear, peeling back the soft tissue of the finger like a glove. That did require some surgery and thereafter a short time in the hospital for fluids and some antibiotics I believe. I later learned that that particular injury was known by the regular emergency personnel as it had happened before.

The actual workday was similar to other medical experiences with an early morning review of each patient, and review of their chart plus a brief work type rounds to briefly discuss all the patients. Usually in the mid-morning there would be a visit to each ward by a higher ranked officer for a sort of formal rounds. These officers were cursory in their examination of the ward and in fact I don't think any of them were medically trained. There was one episode very early in my time on the wards, in fact I believe it was my first day. I think I already alluded to the fact that my group from Boston was in fact a little fun loving and mischievous at times. There were pranksters and jokesters in the group. One of the officers in my group was Dr Kevin McIntyre who was known to me from our regular weekend meetings at the base. He was a clever and very humorous guy known for his quick quips that were often quite funny. Anytime Kevin spoke up, several of us would shut up and listen, expecting to get a laugh. One morning as we were gathering for the expected arrival of the inspecting officer-a Brigadier General -we all could see a group of men gathering at the far end of the ward awaiting the general's arrival to begin rounds. Just about the time that the general entered the room and immediately started his group walking toward us at the front of the ward, Keven inclined slightly to me and whispered: "Let's just discharge all these guys and head to the O club"! That comment in that context was so incongruous that I couldn't help myself and so I had to quickly fake a cough to avoid laughing as the general approached. I was lucky I guess in that I saluted which was acceptable but not usual in the ward setting and this general was gracious, so he told us to be at ease. Those rounds were as expected quite brief.

For some reason that I do not recall, many of us that year at camp had recently read the book: "Catch 22" by Joseph Heller. That is a funny and very zany book that many will remember. It was at the time just really being known and it turned into a classic antiwar and anti-military life type story. It dealt with a bomber group in

World War II stationed on an island I believe off the coast of Italy. The men of the bomber crews were basically frightened by their repeated brushes with near violent death on bombing missions over enemy held territory in Italy. There was a very high loss of planes and men when the planes were seriously damaged or shot down. This kind of nearly daily tension apparently led to all kinds of ways to "blow off steam" and ultimately to all kinds of ways to avoid flying those missions. As I recall, in the book a given pilot or crewman could be so frightened that he would report to the medical group in the hope of being termed unfit for that duty. However, the rules were that being scared to death was not a sign of insanity or some other disability but rather a sign of good mental health since it was really appropriate to be frightened in such circumstances. According to catch 22, a man who sought an excuse from flying these missions because he was crazy could be returned to active duty since being afraid was not at all crazy. I think since this book had just started to really attract attention of so many young men and women and it dealt with a farcical version of military life, it simply was popular in many of the men in my unit. What was really funny and a little nutty was the fact that in many instances, someone would quote a line directly out of this book. Let me provide some examples. In Heller's book, there was one young man who somehow had the duty to sign for the commander every communication sent out whether that be direct written orders, of simply a directive, or even condolence letters to families of those men killed in combat. After all, the commander had many more important things to do, so Ex-pfc Wintergreen signed all documents. There were very many all the time and that job was boring I guess so this man invented ways to provide some kind of variety. He would periodically change the name he used to sign documents-no one really read that anyway. Then he would alter the name at a later time or simply change it entirely in sometimes imaginative ways. So, he might start out signing as "John" but a little later change to "Henry", and then even later sign as "John Henry". Then when he really got desperate, he would sign documents with "Is Anybody in the John, Henry?" This was noted off and on in the book and was always nutty. Another name used in this regard was Washington, or Irving, or simply Washington Irving. Well at summer camp that year, I heard several people quote those kinds of comments and once I was called on the phone and the message was gibberish, so I questioned the caller and he admitted he was Washington. I asked, "Washington who?" and I heard him say Washington Irving as he hung up.

Another small theme in the Heller book that was quoted during my summer camp had to do with a character in the book whose last name was Major. When this man was inducted into military service, the air force computer made some kind of error and so on all his official papers he was listed as Major Major, thus giving this enlisted man an officer rank without any kind of officer training. Being very sensitive to that fact and very uneasy about his actions, this man simply used the system to protect himself from any distress. He instructed his orderly and others to never let anyone in to see him unless he was not there. So, that first year at summer camp there were a few pranks played at times by an elusive person who was said to be Major Major.

I believe it was the Friday of our first week in camp that two of my associates told me there was a plan that night after duty hours to visit the little strip club we had seen on the way into the camp. I appeared less than enthused to these guys, so they pushed a lot and finally I agreed to join them. I finally did admit that I had never been to such a place and didn't really know what to expect. They both assured me that it would be a lot of fun. So we went there and I guess paid to get in. There was a raised stage at one end with a rope like fence on top of the stage edge. There were then many chairs all over a wide expanse of flat floor and I believe on the side of the room some chairs that were set up on top of a raised space. There was piped in loud music and a series of women usually nearly naked who danced around and even sang or at least hummed with the music. The highlight of the night I recall very well, was a woman who called herself Powder Puff. She was topless and danced around with a large white fluffy powder puff complete with powder as she twirled it and tapped herself with it. Finally at the end of her show, she pranced over to the edge of the stage and leaned over the rope. She handed the powder puff to a fellow in the front row and asked if he wanted to powder her boobies. At that point all the guys around this one fellow hooted and hollered and made whistle noises. That was the finale as I recall, and we headed back to the camp and the barracks. I guess that kind of "entertainment" is fairly common around military bases all over the world.

There also were various less risqué types of encounters at camp- for example sometimes there would be movies set up outside and then there also was usually a big party put on by the commanding officer. I think it was in the middle of the first week at camp that year that one night I heard a loud knock on my barracks door. There was a junior officer as I recall at my door who introduced himself and proceeded to tell me that Colonel H. was having a party the next night at the O club for all his officers. He went on to say, " You will be there and you will have a good time!" So, when the time arrived, I did go to the Officers Club and joined the party. I was there a short time and trying to mingle in the crowd when a staff officer approached me and told me that the Colonel wanted me to join him at his table for a drink. Sometime later, I learned that that was in fact a very common situation for every new officer at summer camp. I of course went over to the Colonel's table where he sat with two glasses and a bottle of vodka. As I approached, he reminded me that we were at a totally informal party, and I should relax and have a good time. That of course translated into no need for formal military demeanor or saluting, etc. I was a little nervous, and I think he picked up on that feeling and seemed cordial. He then moved the glasses so they were in front of each of us and poured about 2-3 ounces of vodka into each. He then took his glass and drank most of it before setting it down on the table and looking at me as if to say: "It's your turn, Captain!" Well, it should be obvious that I was in no way that kind of drinker and in fact I had never tasted vodka. I sipped a tiny amount and found that I did not like it. There was no way that I thought I could just drink that liquid down as he had done. I looked at him and told him I was sorry but that I was not a drinker, and I left his table and walked away. I think I was vaguely aware of some whispered comments and possibly a few snickers coming from members of the colonel's staff. One of my associates told me he thought I had made a big mistake by not simply drinking that thing down and acting pleased. Well, I have always wondered about that incident since after the proscribed time in the Army Reserve all the men in my group automatically were advanced to their Majority except me. The officer in charge at that time simply told me he must have mistakenly left my name off that list, and I could take some advanced courses to regain that possible promotion. During my entire time in the Army, I never had any close encounter with the Colonel. I was never aware of any problem in the service for me and was of course never reprimanded.

During that first week at camp most of the days were without any particular concern. We did see a series of minor ailments and injuries. There was one very remarkable event however that started when a 19-year-old enlisted man presented to the emergency room with complaints of sore throat, fever, malaise, and tender lymph nodes mostly in his neck. In the emergency room, this man was noted to have low grade fever and the tender nodes but also a very red throat and his white blood cell count was very high. In addition, these white cells were all bizarre looking lymphocytes, so the thought was that this man had a classic case of infectious mononucleosis. That was a very common infection particularly in young adults. However, when the test was done for that entity, it was negative. That seemed to be somehow in error so it was decided to admit this man for careful observation and so he came to my ward. I repeated a careful exam and also a complete history with no clues of any past significant illness. I looked at the smear of his blood cells in the lab and at least I could tell those were not normal lymphocytes. He was hydrated and seemed a little better with his fever responding to aspirin as I recall. At the time, mononucleosis was still the most likely condition, but I thought what else could this be? It seemed to me that the most serious problem he could have would be acute lymphocytic leukemia. If that was the case, he would be a great risk for several problems including some kind of over whelming infection since his immune system would likely be compromised. So, I decided to go to the pharmacy and see how well we were prepared for some kind of serious infection. I was shocked to discover we were poorly prepared for such a problem as there was only penicillin for IV use and oral tetracycline available. This shed a somewhat different light on this man's illness and our ability to correctly manage it. Several of us discussed this situation and the consensus was that he should be moved to the nearest high intensity medical facility as part of the best approach to his potential problems. That would be the Air Force Base at Rome, New York which was approximately 2-3 hours away from Camp Drum by ambulance. After some discussion, it was decided to transfer my patient and that meant I would go with him in the ambulance with a driver who was also a medical corpsman.

The drive itself was fairly routine and there were no problems in route. I felt a little uneasy sitting in the front of that ambulance as I realized I was basically in command, and I was also green as grass! We did pull up to the entrance to the base and were stopped. I identified us and presented my copy of the printed orders for this trip. Soon the guards indicated we could pass and continue to the base hospital. I did get some verbal directions and we pulled out and into the base itself. The roads were good and two lanes, but we drove for a while and I got uneasy since I had the definite impression that we should have seen the area of the hospital fairly soon. We had made several turns and did end up on a straight road, but it just seemed like too much time had passed and we saw no other vehicles and no sign of a medical facility or parking. Finally we continued on the straight road and there was a long incline so we thought that once we reached the top, we would be able to see a lot better and could find our way. As we neared the top, both the driver and I could see some kind of huge structures reaching high above the level area of the ground. We knew there were planes, and we were looking at the tails high in the air. As we crested that hill, it was obvious we were on the edge of the tarmac of an airfield and there lined up was a series of heavy bombers ready for a potential need. At about the same moment, we heard and then saw two vehicles pull up behind and then to either side of us. These two jeeps stopped and a few soldiers with heavy weapons got out and pointed their weapons at us and I heard a loud voice tell us to remain in the vehicle and then told me to get out with hands raised. I was as they say, "all shook up"! however, certainly complied and then an officer asked me to identify myself and present him with my orders. That was done and we stood there for quite a while before it seemed they relaxed their weapons. I was informed that I had entered a space that was off limits. I thought later these men probably knew who we were since we were in an Army ambulance that had just been passed through the main gate and we did have orders. As I learned gradually, the Rome New York Air Force Base was an active part of the Strategic Air Command with fully armed bombers with nuclear weapons sitting on that tarmac. We were told to follow the lead jeep who led us to the hospital. Once there, a few nurses came out and took control of my patient who was put on a gurney and wheeled through an emergency type facility and into the hospital. We parked the ambulance and entered the emergency area where we were told to take a seat. I think, someone came over and brought us each a cup of coffee while we waited. As everyone would guess, they soon came out and told me that my patient had infectious mononucleosis and their test had proven to be obviously positive. It was decided that the patient would however remain at the base hospital, and we were told to return to our base. That was really a long drive! I called later that week and was told this young man was perfectly fine and was being discharged to his home and family.

After that first week at camp, we were told that our unit would be ordered into the field the next week to set up a base hospital unit. So, I believe on the following Monday we all were gathered in fatigues at the entrance area in front of the hospital and then were loaded on large trucks (the so-called deuce and a half truck) for a convoy out into the deep woods. The trucks were quite roomy and could hold easily 10 or more men with gear. Other vehicles were loaded with the gear we would need as a general field hospital in order to set up a receiving area or emergency ward, hospital beds, a pharmacy of sort, operating rooms, and bunks plus mess type facilities for all personnel. The trucks themselves were huge and the back bed was flat but raised up off the ground with a step type ledge to allow us to climb up. The top and sides were covered with khaki colored heavy cloth and there was a metal back flap on the truck that could be moved up or down as needed. We climbed into the back of these vehicles and sat on benches on each side of the back portion of the truck with a line of us facing inward on each side and thus basically facing each other. There were jeeps and military ambulances also in the convoy that pulled out that morning.

The entire unit then drove off and turned onto an old dirt road deeper into the forest. After some time and it seemed to be possibly thirty minutes there was a loud voice on some kind of loudspeaker I think shouting "Air attack, take cover!" All vehicles pulled to one side of the narrow road, and we were directed to get off the trucks and dive into the brush for cover. At my point in the convoy, there was a small somewhat flat area to one side of the road with tall grass and so I headed there and got down in the weeds. I was probably no more than fifty feet from the truck. Then I heard the sound of a small plane and soon saw it flying overhead and right down the line of the road. I saw some object falling from the plane and it was headed in my direction. As it got near the ground I could see that it was some kind of big bag possibly the size of a large grocery bag. It hit the ground about 15-20 feet from me and there was a large puff of white powder that flew up at the site. At that point, I saw a man in full uniform with a large yellow sash around his torso walking toward me and he said, "You get in the last truck, you are dead!" After a while, the entire group was organized and loaded back onto trucks and several of us were now in a different vehicle at the end of the convoy. That was all the excitement for the day, and we continued on a short time until pulling into a large field with somewhat fewer trees and bushes. This was to be the site of the field hospital. The trucks were unloaded, and the various tents, boxes, and other items unloaded, and the tents were put in position and erected. One of those was simply a large heavy cloth cover that was big enough for a series of collapsible bunks to be lined up along each edge as I recall. This was our sleeping quarters for the week. There also were large tents for an emergency area, pharmacy, headquarters, surgical and medical units plus a ward area with beds for potential patients. I actually was a little bit impressed by the fact that this group of men and women had set up what could be a totally functional hospital in the middle of nowhere. As it turned out, we did see patients trucked in from all over Camp Drum and as far as I knew, we were THE hospital on the base at that time.

All of us fit into Army life and duties fairly well. We did have a lot of free time which many used as a time to read or exercise. That first full night in the forest encampment, I wrote a letter to my wife who I already missed a lot. I also wanted to tell her about some of the events as they were certainly outside of anything she or I ever imagined. I really wish I still had that letter, but it is long gone. I do recall telling Johnny that I had been killed in action that day by a bomb that exploded near where I was sheltering. She obviously knew I was teasing but I did tell her of course that all of that was make believe.

The last night in this encampment was devoted to a huge cook out type party. As I recall there was a trip back to the main base one afternoon for a small group of men in truck or ambulance. The vehicle was driven to a large parking area right near the enlisted men's mess hall. Another vehicle pulled up right next to ours and there was a series of knocks on the side of our ride. The rear door was opened and boxes of medical type gear were removed and then replaced with several large boxes full of T-bone steaks. Thus a system of supply and demand was facilitated and our unit got lots of steaks plus potatoes and bread I believe. Then on the Saturday night before we were to break camp, there was a party of sorts. There were the steaks cooked on a very large makeshift grill with potatoes and an enormous amount of beer. That party lasted all evening and well into the night and everyone had a nice meal and a good time. I remember feeling a full bladder which is no surprise and started heading out of campsite into the adjacent woods to find a suitable place to relieve that pressure. It was fairly dark and as I approached a large tree thinking it would hide me from anyone who might be looking in my direction I loosened my buttons but then heard a voice from down in front of me saying something like, "Not here, Sir!" There was an enlisted man lying at the base of that tree relaxing and he nearly got a warm shower! I found another tree. After a while we all were talked out and full of beer, so the party started to break up. I found my way back to my cot and slept very well until the early morning. There soon was reveille and the day's activities began much as every other day. After shaving and dressing we all gathered for breakfast and after that we were directed to take down all of the tents and start packing up all the gear to go back on the large trucks for the return to base. I saw one deuce and a half parked to one side and when I got to the back of it, I could see the metal back flap was up in its closed position. This formed a rectangular enclosure of good size that was filled to the top with empty beer cans. Once everything was packed into the trucks we all boarded, and the convoy pulled out of that site for the drive back to base. That was an uneventful trip with no low flying planes, etc.

Once back at the main hospital, we simply moved into the previous roles we all played. Within a day we were once again dressed in fatigues and headed back to Boston as our two weeks of active duty were completed. Riding along on that long trip home, I thought about the entire experience with mixed feelings but the number one feeling was my need to see Johnny and little Anne. I did think some of the summer camp did seem a lot like "Catch 22". Afterall, A medical resident was turned into a medical officer in the US Army. He was active in an old and rustic hospital with barracks that could use some paint and then was sent out into deep woods to set up a functioning general hospital. He was symbolically killed in action by a bag of flour dropped from a low flying airplane as a pseudo bomb. Well, I thought: Incongruity reigns!"

There is one more little facet of summer army camp that I want to tell and all those who have gone off to two weeks of summer camp will immediately relate to this part of my story. Once inside the camp, there was an abrupt and pervasive change in language. It seemed to be impossible to complete a sentence without using at least one f word. One example remains in my memory and in fact it happened early on my first week at camp. For some reason, I was speaking with an experienced soldier and in fact he was a sergeant. When I asked him if he was sure, he replied "That's guaran-fucking-teed, sir"! In my conversations with colleagues from the Boston area, they also commented on similar encounters. One of these men did not admit he was speaking about himself but instead told me that he heard from one of his friends the tale of returning home on Sunday from two weeks at camp and his family were all present for a nice dinner. The story goes that his mom, dad, and two sisters, plus one younger brother were at the dinner table when this fellow fresh from camp said: "Pass the fucking butter!". As the story goes, the room became totally silent, and the kids looked at each other with surprise. After a short pause, the dad spoke up and said : "You heard him, pass the fucking butter!" It is certainly true that all of us were bathed in this kind of language for two weeks and it is also true that most of us needed to literally clean up our language before resuming our former positions in medical programs.

As the buses pulled into the base we all could see many cars with people waiting to pick up family members or friends for the drive back to their actual homes. One of those cars was a green VW beetle with my darling wife seated at the steering wheel. Before I was freed to leave, some guy from my group of men stopped by to speak with her and I assume to flirt. She told me later that he approached the side of the car and spoke to her but then seemed to slightly change his attitude when he was close enough to see into her window that she was clearly pregnant! Oh yes, our second baby was in the hatch at that time. I was so glad to see Johnny that I could hardly let go of her. We returned home and picked up Anne who was staying briefly with the Balians across the street. Homecoming is so special! All who read this little memoir will know from their own experiences what a wonderful joy such an event can be. This was then the time in between my house officership and my junior assistant resident year at the Brigham. That second year there would be vastly different from my first year but that is another story for another time.

CHAPTER SEVEN: F Main, The Male Ward

The transition from the Emergency Room to F Main, the male ward, was similar to others but possibly a little less anxiety producing. I was obviously more experienced and had acquired a lot of confidence. Most of the operational plans for evaluation and treatment were well understood and I felt more in command. I also had the thought that somehow taking care of men in the hospital would be easier than women. That was probably true but to only a small degree. As on other transitions, I did visit the F main area a few days before my rotation there just to see the physical plan to gain a small amount of preparation. Since I was leaving the outpatient emergency service, there was no need for me to write lengthy off service notes. I think Johnny also felt something a little different as this was my last rotation as a house officer.

Oh, I still felt some level of apprehension and as the day arrived for me to start there on F Main, I did feel a little anxious and presented myself at the nursing station early in the morning, probably before they expected me. I was given a brief tour and also introduced to several of the nurses. I had a list of the patients already in this unit that I would pick up and so I knew those people would need an introduction by me and for me to carefully read all their charts to be familiar with their potential problems. That first day, I also met Dr Shaun Ruddy who was fully trained in rheumatology and would be my SAR for the entire rotation. He was just like the other SARs, older than me and vastly more experienced but in addition, Shaun was a very warm person and very much down to earth and easy going. I liked him immediately and soon learned that this man was dearly loved by all the nursing personnel because of his manner, caring attitude, and also for his interest in benefit for the nurses as well as the patients.

The F Main ward was all the way at the end of the Pike and so a good distance from the hospital lobby and house staff quarters. Of course this also means F Main was far from cafeteria, labs, x-ray, and emergency ward. As you walked down the Pike to the end, you would encounter a doorway on your left that led into the male ward itself. Once through that doorway, you would see immediately on your right a small single room with a bed, small table, and I believe a small window. That room had several purposes. It was used for the occasional patient who needed isolation from others because of a potentially infectious disease or because a given patient was too disruptive to be out in the main section of the ward. When this room was empty, it served as a nice place to meet with family members of a given patient to answer questions. There were also a few times when this small room was a handy place to put supplies or pieces of equipment to be used a little later and thus the room had a role as a storage site too. I will come back to that in a little while.

As one continued into the ward itself there was a large section on the left that was broken up into small individual beds with cubicle wooden walls and usually some kind of a ventilator. This entire area was basically for respiratory problems and since the ventilators were mostly from the Bird company, we all called the entire area "Bird Land". Continuing on the entrance path one would enter the F Main ward itself. There was a large round room with 13 beds arranged all around the outer edge. The foot of each bed was on the inner side so there was a ring of beds plus a series of pull type curtains suspended from above that could be pulled around a bed to provide a modicum of privacy. During some times when there was a surge of admissions to the hospital, extra beds could be taken out of storage and moved into the actual center of this round room. Portable cloth type covers were mounted in a frame on wheels and could be positioned in between beds for some privacy. I also remember a few times when the hospital was jammed and extra beds would be positioned up against the desk around the nursing station or even underneath a stairwell.

So, on this rotation I would have patients in "Bird Land" and also in the main ward but did not need to leave the ward area except for things like x-ray rounds, or trips to the labs. I still often brought a lunch and snacks from home, because it simply was not practical to run all the way to a cafeteria or sub shop and back when I could eat right at the ward. The day-to-day care was similar to previous comments with early morning work rounds with our SAR and the team of Ralph and I plus a few med students. Often the nurse in charge of a given patient would tag along if she could and that often provided some important bits of information about the night before. A little later in the morning, there were formal teaching rounds given by our attending physician. The patients were men of age approximately 25 to 90 usually. All the ailments that one might imagine were at some time or another represented. Common problems included fevers, infections, bleeding disorders, gastrointestinal complaints, and all sorts of pain. There were also many men admitted with serious problems related to the heavy use of alcohol and there were several admitted with overdose or abuse problems due to various drugs. As I hinted earlier, there were always patients admitted with respiratory problems ranging from clear cut pneumonia to asthma, to coughing up blood, to shortness of breath. Some of the latter group actually had congestive heart failure so the primary defect was cardiac disease rather than respiratory although several men had both.

Very soon after I started on this rotation, there was a very significant but unusual episode in which one of the very large tanks of compressed oxygen somehow fell out of its wheeled receptacle and landed on the floor with a crash. As it struck the floor, the nozzle at its top was struck in such a way as to create a small leak from the tank which was of course under very high pressure. So, the loud crash was immediately followed by a very loud noise of a rushing jet of gas a lot like a jet engine. This jet of gas had a harsh sound with some high-pitched components and the jet itself turned the heavy tank into an agent of destruction. When several of us got to the small room that held that tank, we could see and hear the spinning metal tank banging into the bed and it had already turned the bedside table and a chair into pieces of kindling. It was quite clear that no one could do anything to stop that powerful spinning tank and we were all very happy there had been no patient in that room. A crowd started to gather and after a while, the noise of that jet became less harsh and also less high pitched. After several minutes the tank started to slow down in its spin and finally it stopped. Maintenance men stood back a while and when there was no more sign of a leak, they loaded the tank on some kind of cart and took it away. We could now see that the metal bed frame was dented and bent, and the furniture was no longer of any value. This event was the topic of discussion for the next few days. No one had ever actually seen anything like this episode but there were some stories about similar events with high pressured tanks. From that day onward, all the rest

112

of my life, I always felt a little nervous around similar tanks. That same feeling of vague apprehension comes over me even when I am at home and need to change the propane tank on the bar b que pit.

On this rotation, among other things, I learned how valuable it was to have a man's spouse or significant other present as I obtained the history. So often, a male patient skimmed over details of their problem or even played down some of their symptoms. The female companion would often interrupt and fill in useful details with helpful comments and sometimes they would scold their male counterpart for not telling me the whole story of their illness. Striking examples of this kind of fragmented history included goading the mate into describing how many times he had vomited with blood seen in the vomitus or how he had missed work because of some of his symptoms. I believe all of the house officers and interns everywhere come to realize how often a given male patient would not even have come to the hospital were it not for their significant other. That is certainly something I have observed over and over during my entire medical career. At times, the wife's version of a given illness was quite different from her husband's account. I met the wife of a man I had already admitted, and he had admitted heavy alcohol consumption off and on but recently had severe vomiting that led to hospitalization. The wife filled in details that her husband did not. She told me that he was regularly involved in heavy consumption of bourbon. Over the last few years, she had seen him inebriated, confused, or suffering from what she thought was a hangover. Recently he had come home and appeared intoxicated where upon she berated him, and he went to bed in the mid afternoon. She continued working on dinner preparations which included a whole chicken that she had cut into pieces and rinsed the parts over the sink in a screen bottom pan. As she continued on with other activities to fix dinner, she saw her husband come back into the kitchen a little wobbly. When he reached the sink he could see the uncooked pieces of chicken and he seemed to go into a panic of some sort, so she had a very difficult time calming him down. She told me that it seemed to her that he had seen the parts of the chicken in the sink and somehow thought it was something he had vomited and worse yet, he seemed to think the material in the sink was part of his insides that he had vomited! Certainly, her part of the history added an important component to this man's admission history!

There were as I look back, many admissions because of the ravages of alcohol. There was a time when I admitted an elderly man with fever and shortness of breath who seemed to have a recent onset of illness consistent with pneumonia. I pulled the curtains around this man's bed and started taking my usual detailed history. He and I could hear on the other side of that curtain a doctor that I thought was the neurology resident with a medical student observing his exam on another patient in the next bed. In spite of the need to get my history, I kept being distracted by the comments I heard from the other side of the curtain. My patient was the same way, and I could tell by his expression that he too was somewhat distracted by the happenings on the other side of the curtain. I soon came to the conclusion that the patient on the other side had some kind of encephalopathy as his answers to even basic questions were bizarre. At one point, I and also my patient clearly heard the resident next to us say something like: "Can you see the string I am holding?" From previous experience I knew the resident was at that point holding his thumb and index fingers of both hands up as though he was in fact holding a string. This was a common way to demonstrate when a patient was confabulating. Then the resident said: " OK now make a scissors with your hand and show me how you could cut the string." I assume this was primarily for the benefit of the medical student who would remember forever the scene of a patient seriously confused, with altered thought processes but who still wanted to somehow please his doctor and so he simply agreed to the scenario presented to him. I think I squeezed in one question for my patient before he and I were totally stunned by what that resident said next. We heard him ask his patient "Why do helicopters eat their young?" I looked at my patient and he looked at me as we heard that other patient start to come up with a reason why helicopters might eat their young! The demonstration in the next bed was over and so I could resume my history and physical examination. I think my patient was a little confused but mostly amused by the entire event.

I am a little sad that this memoir is mine and yet I had a large group of colleagues plus 12 other house officers who contributed to my overall story and of course all had experiences of their own. I asked for ideas from those who I could contact, and I have tried to incorporate their thoughts and memories into this memoir. The above comment about history taking for one of my patients with pneumonia brings to mind another similar admission to one of my co house officers-Bruce Chabner. I believe David Livingston was his partner on rotations and he also was present at the time of this episode. An elderly man was hurried up to F Main from the Emergency room with fairly severe pneumonia. This was fairly early in our house officer year. This man was on a monitor and had a large bore IV in place for fluids and medications. He was on an oxygen mask with high flow. As Bruce was trying to settle this patient into his new environment and start to take his history, An IV bottle of fluid containing a large dose of penicillin arrived from the pharmacy. The bottle was connected to the existing IV and opened up to provide its contents to a very sick man. Within only a few minutes, the monitor abruptly changed from sinus tachycardia to complete atrio-ventricular heart block so that the atrial waves on the monitor representing the electrical activity in the upper chambers of the heart continued to be recorded but there were no more ventricular complexes (no QRS complexes) and so there were no actual contractions of the ventricles. So, there was no pulse or blood pressure! These two young physicians took over like champs: David climbed up onto the bed so he could start cardio-pulmonary resuscitation as Bruce lowered the head of the bed and called for help. The nurses brought the crash cart which was always near the nursing station and rapidly connected it to the patient and the wall socket. A crash cart in addition to electrical devices for cardioversion or defibrillation also contained a supply of the drugs that might be needed in an urgent and life-threatening event. As these two colleagues and two nurses prepared for the next steps, someone turned off the IV fluids on the outside chance that somehow that had induced the sudden change in the patient's cardiac electric activity. Very soon a few atrial waves were followed by ventricular waves and that continued to improve so that within a few minutes David could stop pumping on the man's chest as he was back in a normal rhythm with pulses and blood pressure that was acceptable. As they re-assessed this patient it was in fact likely that the IV infusion had played a role. The penicillin was in the form of the potassium salt, and it was thought that the abrupt delivery of potassium might have triggered this man's heart block. The penicillin was restarted cautiously at a slower dose and that was tolerated by the patient with no more rhythm problems. I understand this elderly man did well from then on and did survive. I have no idea if he was ever given a pacemaker, but I bet it was considered. I know that Bruce and David were bonded by that experience. In some ways, that brief episode on F Main typified the house officer experience at the Brigham in those days. You were one minute engrossed in basic care and in the next minute you would be dealing with some severe crisis.

This brings me to a part of my story that is the next thing to unbelievable but as with this entire production, it seems very clear in my memory. Much of this section can be easily confirmed by others who were involved and of course by medical records.

I was well into my rotation on F Main one night when a middle-aged man was admitted to me from the emergency room in severe hepatic (liver) failure. He had a detailed past history of admissions to the Brigham as well as several emergency room visits because of his very serious alcohol habit. On this occasion, he was severely compromised. He was grossly confused, with borderline low blood pressure, a brownish yellow color to his skin, and dirty yellow color to the whites of his eyes. He appeared emaciated and very thin in his face and arms, but he had a slightly prominent and rounded abdomen and puffy feet. The initial laboratory assessment confirmed the gravity of his illness with very high blood level of bilirubin, very high liver enzymes, very low blood albumin(protein) level, and also evidence of some renal failure . As I guessed, his white blood count was also high raising the possibility of some complicating infection which would be a common accompaniment of this kind of admission. Standard initial management was started and efforts to obtain blood, throat, and urine cultures to look for any possible infection. My efforts to obtain any semblance of history like the recent history were to no avail as he was comatose. His wife was there, and she admitted that he had been recently drinking but she did not think it was any more that previous times. He was not employed and had no active interests that I could discover. He had not complained to her about any kind of pain or discomfort, and she was not aware of any falls, injuries, vomiting or diarrhea. There was no history of any kind of bleeding recently. He had not eaten a regular meal in a long time. He was on no regular medications and had no allergies. This man was obviously not my only patient that night, but I did spend most of my time at his bedside. An overall plan of care was formulated, orders written, and I managed to write an admission note and copious progress notes before signing out to Ralph. As I left, I really thought I would not see this patient again.

That night at home, I tried to review what little I had about profound hepatic failure in the few books I had at home. I didn't find much of real interest, but as always, I did feel a sense of remembering a lot that I had learned before. I looked a little haggard I think, and Johnny knew me well by now, so she inquired what was really wrong? I told her a little about this poor man and even a little about his wife. That brief commentary actually led to both of us recalling experiences from our past involving the ravages of alcohol. As a med student I had seen multiple examples of alcohol abuse plus its attendant problems. Johnny had encountered on several occasions as she approached her job, people sitting or lying on the curb out in front of the station. Some seemed to be sleeping, some would ask her for help, but very often there were empty wine bottles nearby in the gutter. She had concluded these people were homeless and that seemed to be the general consensus within the TV station as well. I explained to her that my patient was vastly sicker than the ones she had seen on the street and in fact might not even survive the night. The rest of the night at home was quiet.

I was awake well before the alarm clock sounded and got up shaved and showered and got dressed. Soon I kissed her goodbye, grabbed the lunch she had fixed and was out the door headed for the Brigham and wondering what I would find there. To my pleasant surprise, the patient I had left had survived the night and was not much changed in spite of the initial therapy and fluids. There was no sign of an active infection on any of the cultures, but the man was still comatose with poor response to stimuli. I think several of us were surprised that he had shown no real bleeding with only a weakly positive test for occult blood from each end of his GI tract. Someone, and I think it probably was Shaun, told me that there had been some kind of group meeting during the night about my patient and some consideration of a possible highly experimental new type of care. One of the junior faculty had actually had a period of active research a year before at the Boston City Hospital Department of Surgery working on a system of using a healthy pig liver to detoxify the blood of a sick animal with hepatic failure. I believe this procedure had been done a few times in other labs around the world involving human patients and possibly one or two at the Boston CIty. The procedure involved a connection of blood from a patient with liver failure and very high liver enzymes, bilirubin, etc. directly into the liver of a normal but anesthetized pig. The blood out of the pig's liver was then recirculated back into the human patient. This cross-circulation technique usually resulted in fairly dramatic decrease of all the toxic chemicals in the patient's blood and could therefore lead to a survival in some cases. At least that was what I was told at the time. It is known that the liver has very significant regenerative powers and so it was thought that once the toxins were removed, the normal liver cells would be able to regenerate functioning cells hopefully in sufficient numbers to provide continued life. Within a few hours of starting my day, I was told that in fact an agreement had been reached to transfer my patient to the Boston City hospital for possible trial on a porcine cross circulation treatment. Since this man was technically my patient, I was to accompany him on his trip across the city in an ambulance. The chart with all the lab results and all the x-rays were copied and packaged to go with this patient. The time came for us to leave the Brigham and board the ambulance for the trip to City Hospital. A gurney was wheeled into the male ward by two ambulance attendants. The patient was still semi-comatose and was loaded onto the gurney and secured for transport. I don't recall who was covering for me that night as it was Ralph's night off. I walked alongside the gurney all the way to the hospital ambulance entrance and once the gurney was secured in the vehicle, I got in too. A set of IV poles with hanging bottles were arranged to be secure on turns and the pile of patient records were stored in the underside of the gurney. My memory of that ride is that it was a little chaotic. I don't think we stopped and several times there were sharp turns that left me hanging on to the top of the gurney and the IV poles to maintain an upright position. I think the total ride only took about 20 minutes and soon we passed in front of the Boston City Hospital and the ambulance was put into reverse and backed in and against a sort of loading dock lined up so the opened doors in the back led directly onto that dock. Someone opened the doors and one of the attendants was in the ambulance starting to loosen the attachments that secured the gurney. The records were pulled out and placed on the bed with the patient and we started moving out of the back of that ambulance and onto the dock. I stayed with the patient and the group of us started walking along the length of that dock. There was a long bench on the dock and very many people, some seated. I assumed these were either patients waiting to be seen or possibly friends and family of patients. This was a large group of people but there was one person that I still recall because seeing him was such a shock. This was a young, maybe in his 20's black man and around his neck he wore a leather thong with what looked like a human shrunken head attached. It was small, possibly 3 inches in diameter and freely mobile but still very obvious. I have no idea if that was real or not or where it came from, but the visual image has stuck with me all these years. We continued to move into the hospital and down corridors. I believe there was also a brief elevator ride and soon we wheeled into an empty room. At that point a group of nurses and a resident started to literally take over, moving the patient off the gurney and onto a bed, connecting monitors, and moving the iv poles to a stationary position at the head of the bed. One of the nurses took me aside and quickly went over the patient's recent history and meds and very soon I felt somehow superfluous. The group of transporters gathered, and we were directed back to the ambulance at the dock. Soon we were back at the Brigham, and I returned to my other patients for the rest of that night. That was a busy night, and I did not hear anything about that poor man I had turned over to the team at CIty Hospital. The next evening before I left to go home, I made a few phone calls to the Boston CIty Hospital. After a few tries and one transfer, my call was connected to someone who said he was there and on the team of surgeons. He told me that in spite of everything they could do, my patient had died early in the morning. I didn't get any specific details but was left with the idea that this man was simply too sick for anything to help him. That night I felt strangely numb, but I did tell Johnny all about the transfer of the patient, the ambulance ride, and the scene I found on the emergency dock at the Boston City. I broke my rules about what I would tell her as it all seemed to simply pour out of me, and she didn't say anything. She held me and we just snuggled for a long time. I think we kept little Anne with us in our bed that night or most of it.

The next morning, I was back on duty like nothing unusual had happened. During the early morning, one of the junior faculty came to F main to find me. He said he wanted to talk over what had occurred with my hepatic failure patient. He indicated that he had been the person who had worked with Dr Norman at City Hospital surgical research and had experience with animal-to-animal cross circulation as an experimental way to correct severe toxicity from liver failure. They had done a series of experiments, and some had been fairly successful. Other labs around the world had also done similar work and there had been a few fairly successful trials in human subjects. So, the group in Department of Medicine at the Brigham had discussed this patient of mine and felt it was worth a try. After a long discussion it was decided to transfer my patient over to Boston City for a trial of cross circulation with a pig. He went on to point out that my patient may have actually been too sick for anything to help him. The man was not only acutely sick from hepatic failure due to alcohol, but he was chronically sick with years of alcohol abuse. I got the impression that this fellow was aware of my feelings and was trying to give me some kind of support. He himself was clearly uncomfortable and that is why he wanted to talk to me and why he spent so much time with me. Now that a lot of time has passed and I have had more experience, I can recognize that all of the house officers of my time had also had many unusual and at times nearly experimental management plans to consider and sometimes to try in a highly selective medical education program.

This whole story was at least at times fairly "heavy". That is the way life as house officer or spouse of house officer, or certainly as a patient really was in many cases. But now near the end of this memoir I want to end on some more pleasant memories. One that stands out in my thoughts was the episode on F Main when a small group of the nurses decided to play a little prank on Shaun Ruddy the SAR. I have already indicated that Shaun was a delightful guy, and an excellent leader and teacher who was dearly liked by the nursing staff. His frequent efforts to be sure the nurses were actively involved in all discussions of care served to endear him in their thoughts. In any case, they really loved him and since the rotation was coming to an end, they decided to play a little joke on him. At that time, one of the full-time nurses was well into her pregnancy and it showed. From time to time, Shaun would give her a wink and ask, "How is every little thing?" It may have been her idea, but a plan was hatched to wait until he was all the way at the start of the Pike or even in house staff quarters and then call him urgently and tell him that this nurse had ruptured her membranes on F Main and was in active labor. True to all expectations, Shaun ran all the way to F Main and arrived red faced, out of breath, and excited. At the point of his entry into the ward, the whole group of nurses loudly called out "Just kidding!" It was definitely a brief comic relief and Shaun took it very well.

Somewhere near the final day of our house officership we all were told that Dr Thorn, our chief of medicine, wanted a brief meeting with all of us in the meeting room at the Medicine Department. We all realized he probably wanted to congratulate us for completing the year and wish us well for future plans. My memory of his little talk was something to the effect that we all had completed medical school and acquired a lot of basic knowledge and now we had all completed a vigorous year as house officers with acquisition of enormous amounts of practical experience. With a smile and a twinkle in his eye, he went on to say we were now at a pinnacle of our careers with combination of medical knowledge and clinical experience fresh in our minds and from here on, it would be all downhill!

As I recall, there was a short period between the end of the house officer year and the start of the JAR year that we were off. I know I sat on our front porch and sorted through a full year stack of The New England Journal of Medicine in order to select those articles that I really felt I needed to read. Johnny had dutifully stacked those journals for me as they arrived in the mail. I think there probably was a thin layer of dust in between each of those journals.

All of us were invited to a pool party at the end of our house officership given by General Thomas A Warthin, MD. Dr Warthin had served well in the active US Army and was now retired, and he was the medical director of the West Roxbury VA Hospital. That was an important part of the Brigham experience but none of us would rotate there until our JAR year. At that party we all mixed and enjoyed food and drinks. Some did go swimming. I took a few photos that day and now I can see several very bright colleagues who are no longer living. That of course is not unusual if one considers our house officership was in 1965-1966.

EPILOGUE

More than fifty-seven years have passed since the first day of my house officership at the Peter Bent Brigham Hospital. In the chronicles of scientific progress, that is a very long time, resulting in truly incredible achievements.

On the first day of residency training, I was presented with a beeper so I could be quickly contacted for messages and for all types of patient related information. That small black box on my belt turned out to be a significant harbinger of many changes to come in the general area of rapid communication. The simple beep that alerted me there was information I needed evolved in many ways but did give way to cell phones allowing rapid passage of even detailed messages back and forth plus transmission of photos and video clips. At nearly the same time, computers became more and more useful and led to the internet for vast areas of information on nearly all fields plus enormous ability to store information in the form of brief memos ranging all the way to the contents of an entire library. Little did I know how dramatic all these changes would be and that they would change more or less in tandem with massive changes in the scientific database.

Over those same fifty-seven years, the entire system of medical training would also change. This involved not only physicians and medical students but all of nursing and all categories of medical assistants. Some of the major changes were triggered by public awareness of the possibility that extremely long hours might adversely affect patient management and safety but also could prove to be an impediment to actual learning. Very many changes came about through conscientious individuals on countless committees designed to improve both clinical care and education at a local level or on hospital boards. No doubt, very meaningful changes in the educational methods came about directly due to the role played by major organizations devoted to health care such as The American College of Physicians, The American College of Surgery, The American Medical Association, and the entire system of board certification that developed.

During those same fifty-seven years and starting out as a dedicated but somewhat naïve young physician, I also evolved in search of a career in medicine, cardiology, and teaching. Along the way, I often reflected on the fact that the experiences of my house officer year were stepping stones that I used over and over in solving problems, organizing data, and preparing lectures or bedside teaching. I found myself regularly including comments about the primacy of the patient in any clinical setting and seeking out young physicians who had similar ideals. I especially noted and commented on excellent nurses who also demonstrated that level of real patient care. I recognized that I was very lucky to have already had some of that attitude before finishing medical school but that it was clearly augmented by some of my mentors and teachers. That same principle has guided my entire medical life.

The very rapid growth of science and in particular medical science spurred me on to regularly read journals and the fast growing internet database. In effect, the study habits I learned early in my career blossomed as the associated data base enlarged and so reading and studying continued as lifetime habits. This resulted in me putting together events or patient descriptions from my house officer days with newer developments in medical or cardiovascular management for the specific purpose of planning a lecture. It was remarkable how often I found myself using phrases that sounded like a former teacher and it was very obvious that some of the techniques at examining the cardiovascular system were directly from my early training at the bedside in the Brigham.

The frequent and fairly direct exposure to clinical research during the house officership year plus the understanding of how medical research could very soon affect actual improved patient care led to a side interest for all my professional life. There was a special thrill in conceiving an idea for a potential research project, planning how to get it done, carrying out the entire project, and then writing it up for publication that held at least a part of my career interest. Some of that same feeling would surface at those times when I could help a student or young resident with his or her project or poster presentation.

Looking back on that year of house officership plus all that followed makes me realize this is not just my story, but one that fits in many ways my colleagues from those Boston days. In fact some of the story fits with experiences of very many young graduates of medical schools. As a sample of the kinds of events that transpired after that first year and during the subsequent fifty-seven years I can only offer a few of my own happy events. I did of course, complete the full residency at Peter Bent Brigham Hospital. There were two years of Cardiology Fellowship under Bernard Lown and one year of Cardiac Catheterization training under Charles Sanders at the Massachusetts General Hospital before my SAR year. I was recruited back to St Louis University School of Medicine as an assistant professor of medicine in the Cardiology Division. In 1977 I moved to Columbia, Missouri to accept an Associate Professor role in the University of Missouri Cardiology Division. In 1984 I returned to St Louis as a non-tenured Professor of Medicine at St Louis University School of Medicine and Chief of Medicine and Cardiology at the affiliated SSM St Mary's Hospital. Over a number of years, I did a lot of administrative work as well as teaching and clinical medicine-cardiology. I was deeply gratified by the selection for The Golden Apple Teaching Award both from St Louis U. School of Medicine and the University of Missouri School of Medicine. That award is voted on by the students and therefore has a special significance. I was made a Fellow of the American College of Physicians, The American Heart Association, and the American College of Cardiology. Some time later, I was delighted to accept a Master from the American College of Physicians. I had been by this time elected as Governor of the Missouri Chapter of the ACP, a four year term.

Writing this epilogue required review of the entire story of that one year of training. And so, I was reminded multiple times that I could not have survived that house officer year with long hours, very high intensity patient care, some painful losses and disappointments were it not for my young and very supportive wife, Johnalin. Arriving home after one or two nights away on duty was like a soothing reversal of all my fatigue, anxiety, loss of self confidence, and any hint of depression. Many who read this memoir will relate to the towering strength of love, acceptance, and support that I needed at that time and enjoyed!

Made in the USA
Columbia, SC
17 April 2024

dc3d80ae-7d04-40b7-89ea-6b98ec9f0562R02